# Over thinker's Bible

*A Complete Guide to Managing Your Mind and Finding Inner Peace*

**Philip H. Benjamin**

Overthinker's Bible

*Copyright © 2024 by Philip H. Benjamin*

*All Rights Reserved.*

*No part of this book may be used or reproduced by any means, graphic, electronic, or mechanical, including photocopying, recording, taping, or by any information storage retrieval system without the written permission of the publisher.*

# Overthinker's Bible

# TABLE OF CONTENTS

**Introduction**..................................................................14
- What Is Overthinking?............................................. 14
- How Overthinking Impacts Your Life........................16
- The Goal of This Book: Mastering Your Mind......... 19

**The Overthinker's Mind**..............................................23
- Why Do We Overthink?............................................ 23
- The Neuroscience Behind Overthinking.................. 28
- Common Triggers of Overthinking...........................32

**Types of Overthinking**................................................37
- Rumination vs. Worry: What's the Difference?....... 38
  - Rumination: The Endless Replay of the Past. 38
- Worry: Anticipating the Future................................. 40
- Catastrophizing: Expecting the Worst.....................42
  - How Catastrophizing Works:.......................42
  - Example of Catastrophizing:........................44
- Decision Paralysis: The Fear of Making Choices... 44
  - What Causes Decision Paralysis?...............45
  - Consequences of Decision Paralysis:.........46
- Analysis Paralysis: Thinking Too Much About Every Detail............................................................................47
  - How Analysis Paralysis Develops:..............48
  - Effects of Analysis Paralysis:......................49

## The Overthinking Cycle ............................................. 51
### How Negative Thought Loops Form ...................... 52
#### 1. The Triggering Event: ............................. 52
#### 2. Initial Negative Thought: ....................... 52
#### 3. The Feedback Loop: ............................... 53
#### 4. Escalation of Negative Thoughts: ........... 53
#### 5. Increased Emotional Distress: ................ 54
#### 6. Difficulty in Problem-Solving: .................. 54
### Emotional Triggers and the Snowball Effect ........... 55
#### 1. Identification of Emotional Triggers: ......... 55
#### 2. Amplification of Negative Thoughts: ........ 55
#### 3. The Role of Catastrophizing: ................... 56
#### 4. Cycle of Emotional Responses: ............... 56
#### 5. Inaction and Avoidance: ........................... 57
### The Hidden Role of Anxiety and Fear ..................... 57
#### 1. Anxiety as a Catalyst: .............................. 58
#### 2. Fear of Judgment: .................................... 58
#### 3. Avoidance and Reinforcement: ................ 58
#### 4. The Anxiety-Thought Loop: ..................... 59
#### 5. Coping Mechanisms and Their Effects: ... 59

## Identifying Thought Patterns ................................. 61
### Recognizing Overthinking Habits ........................... 61
#### 1. Monitoring Your Thoughts: ...................... 62
#### 2. Identifying Triggers: ................................. 62
#### 3. Noting Emotional Responses: ................. 63
#### 4. Evaluating Decision-Making Processes: . 63
#### 5. Seeking Feedback from Others: ............. 63
### The Power of Self-Awareness ................................ 64

    1. Enhancing Emotional Intelligence:..........64
    2. Creating a Non-Judgmental Space:........64
    3. Identifying Automatic Thoughts:...............65
    4. Mindfulness Practices:............................65
    5. Setting Intentional Goals:.......................66
Common Cognitive Distortions............................. 66
    1. All-or-Nothing Thinking:......................... 66
    2. Mind Reading:........................................67
    3. Catastrophizing:.................................... 68
    4. Overgeneralization:................................68
    5. Personalization:.................................... 69
    6. Filtering:................................................. 69

**Mindfulness: The Key to Mental Freedom............... 71**
How Mindfulness Works to Stop Overthinking........72
    1. Awareness of Thoughts:........................ 72
    2. Non-Judgmental Observation:................ 72
    3. Anchoring in the Present:.......................73
    4. Reducing Stress Responses:..................73
    5. Enhancing Emotional Regulation:...........74
Easy Mindfulness Practices for Daily Life...............74
    1. Mindful Breathing:..................................75
    2. Body Scan Meditation:...........................75
    3. Mindful Walking:....................................75
    4. Mindful Eating:.......................................76
    5. Five Senses Exercise:........................... 76
Grounding Techniques for Staying Present............ 77
    1. 5-4-3-2-1 Technique:..............................77
    2. Deep Breathing Exercises:..................... 78

3. Grounding Objects: ................................ 78
 4. Affirmations: ........................................... 79
 5. Nature Connection: ................................ 79

**Controlling Your Inner Dialogue ............................ 80**
 Understanding Your Inner Critic ........................... 80
  1. Identifying the Inner Critic: ...................... 81
  2. Origins of the Inner Critic: ...................... 81
  3. Recognizing the Impact: ......................... 82
  4. Challenging the Inner Critic: ................... 82
 Reframing Negative Thoughts .............................. 83
  1. Identify Negative Thoughts: .................... 83
  2. Challenge the Narrative: ........................ 83
  3. Create Alternative Perspectives: ............. 84
  4. Practise Cognitive Distancing: ................ 84
  5. Visualise Positive Outcomes: .................. 84
 Positive Self-Talk and Affirmations ....................... 85
  1. The Importance of Positive Self-Talk: ...... 85
  2. Crafting Effective Affirmations: ............... 85
  3. Repetition and Consistency: ................... 86
  4. Incorporating Affirmations into Daily Life: ... 86
  5. Celebrating Small Wins: ......................... 87

**Cognitive Behavioral Techniques (CBT) for Overthinkers ............................................................. 88**
 Challenging and Replacing Negative Thoughts ..... 88
  1. Identify Negative Thoughts: .................... 89
  2. Question the Validity of Thoughts: .......... 89
  3. Reframe Negative Thoughts: ................... 90
  4. Create a Positive Thought Replacement: ...

90
Thought Records and Journaling............................91
    1. Understanding Thought Records:...........91
    2. Journaling for Self-Reflection:.................92
    3. Daily Gratitude Journals:.......................93
    4. Progress Tracking:.................................93
Behavioural Experiments: Testing Your Thoughts..94
    1. Design Your Experiment:....................... 94
    2. Outline the Hypothesis:..........................94
    3. Conduct the Experiment:...................... 95
    4. Analyse the Results:.............................. 95
    5. Adjust Future Thoughts:.........................95

## Stress and Anxiety Management............................ 97
How Stress Fuels Overthinking.............................. 97
    1. Heightened Sensitivity to Stressors:........ 98
    2. Cognitive Load:....................................... 98
    3. Negative Thought Patterns:.................... 99
    4. Impaired Emotional Regulation:...............99
    5. Physical Symptoms of Stress:................ 99
Relaxation Techniques: Breathing, Meditation, and Visualization........................................................100
    1. Breathing Exercises:............................ 100
    2. Meditation:............................................ 101
    3. Visualisation:........................................102
Developing Healthy Coping Mechanisms............ 103
    1. Physical Activity:................................... 104
    2. Healthy Lifestyle Choices:.....................104
    3. Social Support:.....................................105
    4. Time Management and Organization:...106

       5. Creative Outlets:................................... 107
**The Power of Decision-Making............................... 108**
   Strategies to Make Decisions with Confidence.....109
       1. Clarify Your Goals:................................ 109
       2. Gather Relevant Information:................ 110
       3. Set a Time Limit:................................... 110
       4. Use a Decision-Making Framework:...... 111
       5. Trust Your Instincts:...............................112
       6. Accept Imperfection:............................. 112
   Setting Boundaries with Yourself.......................... 113
       1. Define Decision-Making Parameters:....113
       2. Limit Information Sources:..................... 113
       3. Practice Saying No:...............................114
       4. Create a Decision-Making Routine:....... 115
   How to Stop Seeking Perfection........................... 115
       1. Reframe Your Perspective:................... 115
       2. Set Realistic Standards:........................116
       3. Embrace a Growth Mindset:..................116
       4. Limit Comparison to Others:.................. 117
       5. Practice Self-Compassion:....................118
**Building Mental Resilience......................................118**
   How to Handle Uncertainty................................... 119
       1. Embrace the Unknown:..........................119
       2. Practice Mindfulness:............................120
       3. Limit Information Overload:....................121
       4. Develop Contingency Plans:..................122
       5. Connect with Support Networks:...........123
   Cultivating Optimism and a Growth Mindset.........123

1. Practice Gratitude: ............................... 124
2. Reframe Challenges: ........................... 125
3. Surround Yourself with Positivity: ......... 125
4. Embrace Lifelong Learning: .................. 126
Strengthening Emotional Intelligence ................ 127
1. Enhance Self-Awareness: ..................... 127
2. Manage Emotions: ............................... 128
3. Improve Empathy: ................................ 129
4. Build Strong Relationships: ................... 130

**Developing Focus and Clarity ............................ 131**
How to Prioritise What Really Matters ............... 132
1. Identify Your Core Values: ..................... 133
2. Use the Eisenhower Matrix: ................... 133
3. Set SMART Goals: ................................ 134
4. Break Tasks into Smaller Steps: ............ 135
5. Regularly Review and Adjust Priorities: 136
Time Management for a Clearer Mind ................ 136
1. Create a Daily Schedule: ....................... 137
2. Use Time Management Techniques: ..... 137
3. Limit Distractions: .................................. 138
4. Learn to Say No: ................................... 139
5. Reflect on Time Usage: ......................... 140
The Art of Letting Go .......................................... 140
1. Identify What to Let Go: ......................... 141
2. Practice Acceptance: ............................ 141
3. Use Mindfulness Techniques: ............... 142
4. Replace Negative Habits with Positive Ones: ...................................................... 143
5. Celebrate Your Progress: ..................... 143

**Finding Peace in the Present................................... 144**
  Gratitude Practices to Calm Your Mind................. 145
    1. Daily Gratitude Journaling:..................... 146
    2. Gratitude Meditation:............................. 147
    3. Express Gratitude to Others:................ 147
    4. Create a Gratitude Jar:......................... 148
    5. Gratitude Walks:................................... 148
  How to Surrender Control and Embrace the Unknown............................................................. 149
    1. Acknowledge Your Need for Control:.... 150
    2. Practice Mindfulness:............................ 150
    3. Reframe Your Perspective:................... 151
    4. Set Intentions Instead of Expectations:. 152
    5. Seek Support:....................................... 153
  Living a Life of Purpose Beyond Overthinking...... 153
    1. Explore Your Passions:.......................... 154
    2. Define Your Values:............................... 154
    3. Set Meaningful Goals:........................... 155
    4. Cultivate a Growth Mindset:.................. 156
    5. Practice Self-Compassion:.................... 156

**Sustaining Mental Clarity......................................... 158**
  Daily Habits for a Clear Mind................................ 158
    1. Mindful Mornings:.................................. 159
    2. Prioritising Tasks:................................... 159
    3. Digital Detox:......................................... 160
    4. Breaks and Downtime:.......................... 161
  Building a Routine for Mental Wellness................ 161
    1. Establish a Consistent Wake-Up and Sleep Schedule:......................................... 162

    2. Incorporate Physical Activity:................ 162
    3. Schedule Time for Reflection:............... 163
    4. Designate "Me Time":........................... 164
  The Role of Sleep, Nutrition, and Exercise........... 164
    1. Sleep: The Foundation of Mental Clarity..... 165
    2. Nutrition: Fueling the Brain................... 166
    3. Exercise: The Mind-Body Connection...166

**Overcoming Setbacks.............................................167**
  How to Handle Relapses into Overthinking.......... 168
    1. Acknowledge Your Feelings:..................169
    2. Use Mindfulness Techniques:............... 169
    3. Reframe Your Thoughts:....................... 170
    4. Take Action:........................................ 171
  Learning from Failure and Moving Forward..........172
    1. Embrace a Growth Mindset:................. 172
    2. Reflect on the Experience:.....................173
    3. Develop an Action Plan:.......................173
  Celebrating Your Progress...................................174
    1. Acknowledge Achievements:................ 174
    2. Keep a Success Journal:...................... 175
    3. Share Your Journey:............................ 176

**Daily Mindfulness Prompts................................. 177**
  Prompts for Emotional Awareness...................... 179
  Prompts for Gratitude......................................... 180
  Prompts for Self-Awareness and Reflection......... 181
  Prompts for Staying Present................................182
  Prompts for Mindful Breathing and Grounding..... 183
  Prompts for Stress and Anxiety Management...... 184

**Overthinker's Bible**

Prompts for Personal Intentions and Goals.......... 186
Prompts for Relationships and Connections......... 187
Prompts for Self-Love and Compassion............... 189
Prompts for Letting Go and Moving Forward........ 190
Prompts for Mindful Living................................... 192

**Overthinker's Bible**

# Introduction

## What Is Overthinking?

Overthinking is the mental habit of dwelling on a single thought or set of thoughts for an excessive amount of time. It can involve endlessly analysing situations, second-guessing decisions, and imagining worst-case scenarios, even when there's little reason to worry. Overthinking often feels like being trapped in a mental loop, where the same thoughts and worries play on repeat, consuming your mental energy without producing solutions. It's not just about thinking too much; it's about thinking in a way that is unproductive and ultimately harmful to your well-being.

There are two main types of overthinking: **rumination** and **worry**. Rumination involves obsessing over the past — reliving mistakes, missed opportunities, or embarrassing moments, and analysing them from every possible angle. Worry, on the other hand, is more future-focused. It's the habit of imagining potential problems, often in exaggerated forms, and trying to solve them before they even arise. Both types of overthinking trap you in a cycle of mental stress, preventing you from living in the present.

While overthinking can sometimes be mistaken for problem-solving, it's important to understand the distinction. Problem-solving involves actively looking for solutions, while overthinking focuses more on the problem itself, often without any clear or constructive goal. Overthinkers often feel like they are accomplishing something by mentally exhausting every possibility, but in reality, they are merely spinning their wheels in place.

## How Overthinking Impacts Your Life

Overthinking is more than just a mental annoyance; it can have far-reaching effects on various aspects of your life. Whether it's impacting your personal relationships, professional productivity, or overall mental health, the toll of overthinking can be substantial.

One of the most significant ways overthinking impacts your life is by robbing you of peace of mind. Instead of experiencing moments of calm, your brain is constantly racing, analysing everything from trivial details to major life decisions. This mental noise can create a chronic state of anxiety, as your mind is always "on," unable to relax or focus on what truly matters.

**Emotional stress** is a direct consequence of overthinking. When you constantly replay scenarios, criticise yourself for past mistakes, or anticipate future disasters, you put yourself in a perpetual state of worry. This stress can manifest physically as well, contributing to headaches, insomnia, fatigue, and even more severe health issues like high blood pressure or heart disease. Over time, this prolonged state of mental stress can erode your emotional resilience, making it harder to deal with everyday challenges.

In **personal relationships**, overthinking can create tension. You may find yourself analysing every word, text, or action from a loved one, convinced that their behaviour has hidden meanings or ulterior motives. This can lead to unnecessary arguments, misunderstandings, and distance, as your partner, friend, or family member may feel like they're walking on eggshells around you.

**Decision paralysis** is another major consequence. Overthinkers often struggle to make decisions because they fear making the wrong choice. They weigh every option, anticipate every potential outcome, and, as a result, find it nearly impossible to commit to anything. This paralysis can impact both small decisions, like what to eat for dinner, and major life choices, like career moves or relationships. It leads to missed opportunities, a sense of helplessness, and regret.

Overthinking also **stifles creativity** and productivity. When your mind is cluttered with an overabundance of thoughts, it becomes difficult to focus on a single task. Your brain is too preoccupied with what-ifs, worst-case scenarios, and overanalysis, preventing you from working efficiently. This constant mental fog can delay progress, hinder innovation, and cause you to feel overwhelmed by tasks that might otherwise be manageable.

Ultimately, overthinking prevents you from living fully in the present. By keeping you stuck in the past or worrying about the future, it robs you of the ability to enjoy the moment. You miss out on experiences, joys, and opportunities that only exist when you're fully engaged in the now. The more time you spend in your head, the less time you spend truly living.

## The Goal of This Book: Mastering Your Mind

The primary goal of *Overthinker's Bible* is to provide you with the tools and knowledge necessary to break free from the cycle of overthinking. Through understanding the mechanisms of your mind, recognizing unproductive thought patterns, and applying practical strategies, you'll learn to regain control over your mental space and find the inner peace you've been missing.

Overthinking is not something that will vanish overnight, but by committing to the process of mental mastery, you can significantly reduce its impact on your life. This book will guide you step by step through the journey of self-awareness, mindfulness, and action, giving you the resources you need to make lasting changes. Whether you're someone who over analyse every detail or struggles with making decisions, this book is tailored to help you manage those tendencies.

You'll discover how to shift your focus from endless rumination to productive problem-solving. The emphasis will be on cultivating mindfulness, learning to live in the present moment, and reframing your thoughts in a way that promotes clarity and calm rather than stress and confusion.

Moreover, this book will help you understand that mastering your mind is not about shutting down your thoughts but about developing a healthy relationship with them. It's about learning to recognize when your thoughts are helpful and when they're holding you back. By the end, you'll have a set of mental tools that you can use to navigate life's challenges with confidence and peace.

Mastering your mind isn't just about stopping overthinking—it's about creating mental clarity, focus, and emotional resilience that will allow you to live a more fulfilled and present life. Each chapter will offer practical tips, exercises, and techniques that you can apply in your daily routine to gradually break free from the grip of overthinking and take back control of your mental and emotional well-being.

In *Overthinker's Bible*, you're not only going to learn how to stop overthinking, but also how to

**Overthinker's Bible**

foster a mindset that supports inner peace, productivity, and joy. With time, practice, and patience, you'll move from being an overthinker to mastering your thoughts—and ultimately, your life.

# The Overthinker's Mind

Overthinking is a pervasive mental habit that affects millions of people. It involves analysing, rehashing, and worrying about situations, often in an unproductive and distressing manner. For overthinkers, even the simplest decisions can become overwhelming, and every thought can spiral into a cascade of anxiety and doubt.

## Why Do We Overthink?

At its core, overthinking is a response to uncertainty, fear, and the desire for control. It's the brain's attempt to solve a perceived problem, even when no immediate solution is necessary or possible. While occasional reflection or analysis can be productive, overthinking goes beyond that — it traps us in a cycle of mental rumination that produces no real outcomes, leading instead to stress, anxiety, and mental exhaustion.

Here are some of the key reasons why people tend to overthink:

1.  **Fear of the Unknown**
    Uncertainty is a breeding ground for overthinking. When we don't have all the answers, our minds try to fill in the gaps by imagining worst-case scenarios. This is especially true in situations where we feel we have little control, like waiting for a medical diagnosis, wondering if we'll get a job offer, or worrying about how others perceive us. Overthinkers often believe that by analysing every possible outcome, they can prepare for any eventuality. However, this endless mental exercise only creates more anxiety, as it often leads

to catastrophic thinking — the assumption that the worst-case scenario is the most likely outcome.

2. **Need for Control**

   Many overthinkers have a deep-seated need for control. When faced with uncertainty, they attempt to regain a sense of mastery by thinking through every possible angle. They believe that if they can foresee every obstacle or problem, they can prevent negative outcomes. This drive for control often backfires, as overanalyzing situations leads to decision paralysis, frustration, and a feeling of being out of control.

3. **Perfectionism**

   Overthinkers often set impossibly high standards for themselves. They worry about making mistakes, disappointing others, or not living up to their own expectations. As a result, they over analyse every choice they make, fearing that a single misstep could lead to failure or embarrassment. This perfectionist mindset fuels overthinking by making people believe that there is always a "right" answer or "perfect" outcome, and if they just think hard enough, they'll find it.

4. **Fear of Failure or Rejection**
   The fear of failure or rejection often leads to overthinking. People become obsessed with anticipating negative outcomes, and instead of taking action, they get stuck in a loop of indecision and worry. For example, someone might overthink before asking for a promotion at work, thinking of all the ways their request could be denied or lead to criticism. This fear-driven overanalysis often prevents people from taking risks or pursuing opportunities that could benefit them.

5. **Past Trauma or Negative Experiences**
   People who have experienced trauma, loss, or significant negative experiences are often more prone to overthinking. Their minds may be conditioned to replay painful memories or analyse how they

could have done things differently. Over time, this can create a pattern of rumination, where the person replays old mistakes or bad outcomes in an attempt to prevent future pain. Unfortunately, this focus on the past only leads to more distress in the present.

6. **Anxiety and Mental Health Issues**
Anxiety and overthinking are often deeply intertwined. For those with generalised anxiety disorder (GAD), obsessive-compulsive disorder (OCD), or other mental health conditions, overthinking can be a constant companion. Anxiety drives the brain to focus on potential threats or worries, leading to incessant overanalysis. In these cases, overthinking is not just a habit — it's a symptom of a deeper psychological issue that requires intervention.

## The Neuroscience Behind Overthinking

The brain is a powerful organ, designed to help us analyse, plan, and make decisions. However, when these cognitive functions are overused, they can lead to overthinking. To understand why overthinking happens, it's important to look at the brain's structure and how it processes thoughts.

1. **The Prefrontal Cortex: The Thinker's Playground**
   The prefrontal cortex (PFC) is the part of the brain responsible for higher-level thinking, decision-making, and planning. It's the area that allows us to reflect on past experiences, weigh options, and anticipate future events. While the PFC is essential for rational thought, it can also be the source of overthinking. When overthinkers engage this part of the brain too much, they get caught in a loop of

analysis without ever reaching a conclusion.

2. **The Amygdala: The Brain's Fear Center**
The amygdala, located deep within the brain, is responsible for processing emotions, particularly fear and anxiety. When faced with uncertainty or perceived threats, the amygdala kicks into overdrive, triggering a "fight or flight" response. For overthinkers, the amygdala can exacerbate feelings of anxiety and worry, fueling the cycle of overanalysis. The constant activation of the amygdala keeps the brain on high alert, making it difficult to relax or stop the flow of thoughts.

3. **Overactivity in the Default Mode Network (DMN)**
The Default Mode Network (DMN) is a collection of brain regions that become active when we are not focused on the outside world — essentially when our minds are at rest or wandering. Research suggests that overactivity in the DMN is

linked to rumination and overthinking. In overthinkers, the DMN may be hyperactive, causing them to continuously rehash past events or worry about the future, even when they're trying to relax or focus on something else.

4. **Cortisol and the Stress Response**
Overthinking often triggers the release of cortisol, the stress hormone. When the brain perceives a threat — even if it's just a worry about something that might happen — the body releases cortisol to prepare for a stressful situation. Over time, high levels of cortisol can impair memory, decision-making, and emotional regulation, leading to even more overthinking. This creates a feedback loop: stress leads to overthinking, which leads to more stress.

5. **Neuroplasticity: Rewiring the Overthinker's Brain**
Neuroplasticity is the brain's ability to reorganise itself by forming new neural connections throughout life. This means

that the more you engage in a particular thought pattern, the more your brain becomes wired to repeat that pattern. Overthinkers essentially train their brains to overanalyze by repeatedly engaging in overthinking. However, neuroplasticity also means that you can rewire your brain to adopt healthier thinking habits. With practice, you can train your brain to break free from the cycle of overthinking and develop more balanced thought processes.

## Common Triggers of Overthinking

While overthinking is often an internal mental process, it is typically triggered by external or emotional factors. Recognizing these triggers is the first step in learning how to manage and reduce overthinking.

1. **Uncertainty and Ambiguity**
   When faced with unclear situations, overthinkers tend to fill in the blanks with

worst-case scenarios. Whether it's waiting for the results of a medical test, uncertainty in relationships, or ambiguity at work, the lack of clear answers often triggers a spiral of overanalysis. Overthinkers crave certainty and control, and when these are lacking, their minds go into overdrive.

2. **Big Life Decisions**
Major decisions — such as choosing a career path, moving to a new city, or entering a serious relationship — are prime triggers for overthinking. The stakes feel high, and overthinkers often struggle with the fear of making the wrong choice. This can lead to decision paralysis, where they are unable to move forward because they're stuck in a loop of weighing every possible outcome.

3. **Social Situations**
Social interactions can trigger overthinking, especially for those who are self-conscious or have social anxiety. Overthinkers may replay conversations in

their heads, worrying about what they said, how they were perceived, or whether they made a good impression. This can lead to a constant state of self-criticism and doubt.

4. **Past Mistakes or Regrets**
People who tend to dwell on their past are more prone to overthinking. Whether it's a failed relationship, a mistake at work, or a missed opportunity, overthinkers often replay these events in their minds, analysing what they could have done differently. This rumination keeps them stuck in the past, preventing them from moving forward.

5. **Fear of Judgment or Criticism**
Overthinkers often worry about how others perceive them. Whether it's fear of judgement from peers, family, or colleagues, this concern about external opinions can trigger a cycle of overanalysis. Overthinkers may spend hours second-guessing their actions or words, worrying that they've said

something wrong or made a bad impression.
6. **High Expectations and Pressure**
When people set unrealistic expectations for themselves, it can lead to intense overthinking. Overthinkers often pressure themselves to achieve perfection, whether it's in their careers, relationships, or personal goals. This pressure to be perfect can make even small tasks feel overwhelming, leading to endless cycles of doubt and self-criticism.

# Types of Overthinking

Overthinking manifests in various forms, each with its own distinct patterns and consequences. Understanding the different types of overthinking is crucial for recognizing how it affects our daily lives and mental well-being. Here, we explore four key types of overthinking: **rumination**, **worry**, **catastrophizing**, and **decision paralysis**, and we also explain how these patterns disrupt a person's ability to function and make clear decisions.

## Rumination vs. Worry: What's the Difference?

At first glance, **rumination** and **worry** may seem like two sides of the same coin, both involving persistent, repetitive thoughts. However, they are distinct in their focus, direction, and emotional impact. While both can be detrimental, understanding the difference between them can help in addressing the specific thought patterns that dominate an overthinker's mind.

**Rumination: The Endless Replay of the Past**

Rumination refers to the act of dwelling on past experiences, particularly negative events or outcomes. It's a mental process where the mind becomes trapped in a loop of replaying what has already happened, often with the goal of understanding or "fixing" the past. People who ruminate may think about past mistakes, missed opportunities, or painful situations, constantly analysing what went wrong or what they should have done differently.

### Key Characteristics of Rumination:

- **Focus on the Past:** Rumination revolves around events that have already taken place, often centering on perceived failures, mistakes, or regrets.
- **Self-Criticism:** Overthinkers who ruminate frequently criticise themselves for their past actions or inactions, creating feelings of guilt or shame.
- **Lack of Resolution:** The mind keeps cycling through the same thoughts without reaching any productive conclusion or solution, which can lead to prolonged emotional distress.
- **Emotional Impact:** Rumination is closely associated with depression and low self-esteem, as the constant replay of negative events reinforces feelings of hopelessness and helplessness.

## Worry: Anticipating the Future

Worry, on the other hand, is a form of overthinking that focuses on future events, particularly those that might go wrong. When people worry, they anticipate negative outcomes or worst-case scenarios, often imagining potential threats or challenges. Unlike rumination, which is stuck in the past, worry is forward-looking and deals with uncertainty about what might happen next.

**Key Characteristics of Worry:**

- **Focus on the Future:** Worry involves thoughts about potential problems or dangers that have yet to occur. Overthinkers constantly anticipate what could go wrong in various situations.
- **Anxiety and Fear:** Worry is closely linked to anxiety, as it feeds on the fear of the unknown and the unpredictability of the future. It can range from mild concerns to overwhelming fears.
- **Attempt to Control Outcomes:** People who worry often believe that by thinking through all possible negative outcomes, they can somehow prevent or prepare for them. However, this is rarely effective, as

many future events are beyond their control.
- **Physical Symptoms:** Chronic worry can lead to physical symptoms such as increased heart rate, muscle tension, headaches, and insomnia, all related to heightened stress levels.

# Catastrophizing: Expecting the Worst

Catastrophizing is a particularly destructive form of overthinking where a person jumps to the worst possible conclusion, even when there is little evidence to support it. It involves imagining that the most extreme and negative outcome will occur in any given situation, which leads to heightened anxiety and fear.

### How Catastrophizing Works:

When a person catastrophizes, they may start with a small, relatively manageable problem but quickly escalate their thinking to an exaggerated and highly negative scenario. For instance, if someone receives a critical email at work, their mind may immediately jump to fears of losing their job, financial ruin, and personal failure — even though the actual situation may be minor.

## Key Features of Catastrophizing:

- **Exaggeration:** The hallmark of catastrophizing is blowing situations out of proportion. A minor issue is seen as a catastrophe, leading to intense fear and panic.
- **Worst-Case Scenarios:** Overthinkers who catastrophize frequently fixate on worst-case outcomes, believing that these extreme scenarios are not only possible but likely.
- **Anxiety Amplifier:** Catastrophizing feeds directly into anxiety. The belief that disaster is imminent keeps the mind in a heightened state of alert, constantly scanning for potential threats.
- **Negative Spiral:** Once someone begins to catastrophize, it's easy for their thinking

to spiral downward. One negative thought leads to another, creating a chain of disastrous possibilities that leave the person feeling helpless and overwhelmed.

**Example of Catastrophizing:**

Imagine a student who fails one exam. Instead of seeing this as an isolated event, they catastrophize by believing it means they'll fail the entire course, drop out of school, and never find a good job. This type of thinking can paralyse the individual with fear and stress, even though the likelihood of such extreme outcomes is very low.

---

# Decision Paralysis: The Fear of Making Choices

**Decision paralysis**, or **indecision**, occurs when someone becomes overwhelmed by the prospect of making a choice, no matter how small or significant. Overthinkers in this state spend so much time analysing and weighing the pros and cons of each option that they are unable to make a decision at all. This form of overthinking can affect everything from minor daily choices, such as what to wear or what to eat, to life-altering decisions like choosing a career path or ending a relationship.

**What Causes Decision Paralysis?**

- **Fear of Making the Wrong Choice:** One of the most common reasons for decision paralysis is the fear of regret. Overthinkers often worry that if they make the wrong decision, they'll suffer negative consequences, and they won't be able to undo their mistake. This fear can be paralysing, leading them to avoid making any decision at all.
- **Overwhelming Options:** Decision paralysis is often exacerbated by too many choices. When faced with a wide range of options, overthinkers may become trapped in an endless cycle of comparing and contrasting, afraid of missing out on the "best" choice.

- **Perfectionism:** Overthinkers often believe that there is one "right" or "perfect" decision to be made, and anything less than that is unacceptable. This leads to endless deliberation and second-guessing.

**Consequences of Decision Paralysis:**

- Missed Opportunities: The inability to make decisions can result in lost opportunities. When overthinkers wait too long to act, they may miss deadlines, opportunities, or other chances that could have benefited them.
- **Regret and Self-Blame:** Ironically, the very fear that prevents people from making decisions — the fear of regret — often leads to regret when opportunities pass by.
- **Low Self-Esteem:** Constantly second-guessing oneself can erode confidence, making it harder to trust one's instincts or judgments in the future.

## Analysis Paralysis: Thinking Too Much About Every Detail

**Analysis paralysis** is a form of overthinking where a person becomes so absorbed in analysing every possible aspect of a situation that they are unable to make progress or take action. This occurs because they are trapped in a loop of thinking and rethinking every detail, to the point where they cannot move forward.

**How Analysis Paralysis Develops:**

Analysis paralysis often arises from the desire to make the "best" or "most informed" decision. Overthinkers feel the need to gather every piece of information available before making a choice or moving ahead with a plan. However, the sheer volume of information and options can overwhelm them, leading to inaction.

**Key Features of Analysis Paralysis:**

- **Overabundance of Information:** With the advent of the internet and modern technology, people have access to more information than ever before. Overthinkers may fall into the trap of endlessly searching for additional data, believing that with just a little more research, they'll finally have enough to make a decision.
- **Perfectionism:** As with decision paralysis, perfectionism plays a significant role in analysis paralysis. The desire to be absolutely certain of every aspect of a situation leads to excessive analysis, which prevents progress.
- **Fear of Uncertainty:** Overthinkers caught in analysis paralysis often believe that if they think through every possible detail, they'll be able to predict and control the outcome. However, this need for certainty is unattainable, and the desire for complete control leads to inaction.

**Effects of Analysis Paralysis:**

- **Inaction and Stagnation:** When people spend too much time analysing, they often fail to make progress. Whether it's a work project, personal goal, or even a simple decision, overanalyzing prevents them from moving forward.
- **Missed Deadlines and Opportunities:** Analysis paralysis can cause people to miss important deadlines or opportunities because they spend too much time in the planning phase without executing their ideas.
- **Frustration and Burnout:** Constantly thinking and rethinking every detail can be mentally exhausting, leading to frustration, burnout, and a sense of defeat.

# The Overthinking Cycle

The overthinking cycle is a complex interplay of thoughts, emotions, and behaviours that can trap individuals in a continuous loop of excessive rumination and worry. Understanding this cycle is essential for breaking free from its constraints and cultivating a healthier mindset. Below, we explore how negative thought loops form, the emotional triggers that amplify them, and the hidden roles of anxiety and fear in perpetuating overthinking.

## How Negative Thought Loops Form

Negative thought loops are recurring patterns of thinking that reinforce negative beliefs and feelings. These loops often start with a triggering event—an experience or thought that ignites overthinking. From there, the cycle can spiral out of control, creating a self-sustaining loop that is difficult to escape.

**1. The Triggering Event:**

The cycle typically begins with a specific trigger, which can be external (e.g., an argument, a missed opportunity) or internal (e.g., a self-critical thought). This event serves as the catalyst for overthinking, leading to an initial wave of negative thoughts.

**2. Initial Negative Thought:**

Once the trigger occurs, an individual may experience a rush of negative thoughts. These thoughts often revolve around self-doubt, fear, or anxiety related to the triggering event. For instance, after receiving constructive criticism, someone might think, "I always mess up. I'm a failure."

### 3. The Feedback Loop:

As these initial thoughts take hold, they prompt further negative thinking. This feedback loop intensifies the emotional response, leading to more ruminative thoughts. For example, the thought of being a failure can lead to memories of past mistakes, which further reinforces the belief of inadequacy.

### 4. Escalation of Negative Thoughts:

With each iteration of the loop, the intensity of negative thoughts escalates. The mind becomes entrenched in this cycle, focusing on worst-case scenarios and amplifying feelings of helplessness. Individuals may become hyper-aware of potential dangers or mistakes, further fueling the overthinking.

### 5. Increased Emotional Distress:

As the cycle continues, the emotional distress becomes more profound. Feelings of anxiety, sadness, or frustration can intensify, making it even harder to break free from the loop. The individual may feel trapped in their thoughts, leading to exhaustion and overwhelm.

**6. Difficulty in Problem-Solving:**

Ironically, while overthinking often stems from a desire to solve problems, it can lead to a state of mental paralysis. The individual becomes so preoccupied with analysing every angle that they struggle to arrive at any constructive solution, perpetuating the cycle.

---

# Emotional Triggers and the Snowball Effect

Emotional triggers play a pivotal role in the overthinking cycle. These triggers can originate from personal experiences, interactions with others, or even social situations. Understanding how they contribute to the snowball effect of overthinking can illuminate pathways for change.

**1. Identification of Emotional Triggers:**

Emotional triggers are specific stimuli that evoke strong emotional responses. They can be words, situations, or even memories that elicit feelings of insecurity, sadness, or anxiety. For example, a comment about someone's appearance might trigger deep-seated insecurities about body image.

**2. Amplification of Negative Thoughts:**

Once an emotional trigger is activated, it can lead to an immediate influx of negative thoughts. The individual may begin to question their worth, leading to further introspection. This can create a snowball effect where each negative thought reinforces the next.

**3. The Role of Catastrophizing:**

As negative thoughts amplify, the tendency to catastrophize becomes stronger. This means the individual might jump to extreme conclusions about their abilities or future outcomes based on their emotional reactions. A small mistake at work might lead to fears of job loss, triggering a cascade of worry and anxiety.

**4. Cycle of Emotional Responses:**

The more the individual engages with these negative thoughts, the stronger their emotional responses become. Feelings of anxiety can lead to physical symptoms such as tension, fatigue, or even panic attacks, further entrenching them in the overthinking cycle.

**5. Inaction and Avoidance:**

As the emotional turmoil increases, individuals may resort to avoidance behaviours to cope with their distress. This can include procrastination, withdrawing from social situations, or avoiding decisions altogether. Such avoidance only reinforces the cycle, as it prevents the individual from addressing the initial trigger or taking constructive action.

---

# The Hidden Role of Anxiety and Fear

Anxiety and fear are central to the overthinking cycle, acting as both catalysts and products of excessive rumination. These emotions can create a feedback loop that exacerbates overthinking and reinforces negative thought patterns.

**1. Anxiety as a Catalyst:**

Anxiety often serves as the initial spark for overthinking. The fear of the unknown or of making mistakes can lead individuals to overanalyze situations in an attempt to control outcomes. This anxiety can be situational (related to a specific event) or generalised (persistent worry about various aspects of life).

**2. Fear of Judgment:**

Fear of judgement from others can exacerbate overthinking. Individuals may worry about how they are perceived, leading to self-doubt and second-guessing their actions. This fear can prevent them from expressing their thoughts or making decisions, further entrenching the cycle.

**3. Avoidance and Reinforcement:**

As anxiety and fear grow, individuals may avoid situations that trigger these emotions. This avoidance provides temporary relief but ultimately reinforces the fear. For example, if someone avoids social situations due to anxiety about being judged, they may miss opportunities for connection, leading to feelings of loneliness and further anxiety.

**4. The Anxiety-Thought Loop:**

The relationship between anxiety and negative thoughts creates a vicious cycle. Anxiety breeds negative thoughts, which in turn amplify anxiety. For example, worrying about a presentation can lead to thoughts of inadequacy, which then heightens anxiety about performing poorly. This cycle can become self-sustaining and difficult to break.

**5. Coping Mechanisms and Their Effects:**

Individuals often resort to unhealthy coping mechanisms, such as substance use or excessive reliance on distraction techniques, to manage their anxiety. While these may provide short-term relief, they do not address the root causes of overthinking and can perpetuate the cycle in the long run.

# Identifying Thought Patterns

Identifying thought patterns is a crucial step in overcoming overthinking and cultivating a healthier mindset. By recognizing the habits that contribute to overthinking, individuals can develop greater self-awareness and challenge cognitive distortions that perpetuate negative thinking.

## Recognizing Overthinking Habits

Recognizing overthinking habits involves becoming aware of specific thoughts and behaviours that lead to excessive rumination and worry. This self-awareness is essential for breaking free from the overthinking cycle.

**1. Monitoring Your Thoughts:**

To identify overthinking habits, start by paying attention to your thought processes throughout the day. Keep a journal or use a note-taking app to jot down thoughts that arise, particularly in response to stress or uncertainty. Look for patterns in your thinking, such as repetitive questions or themes.

**2. Identifying Triggers:**

Recognize the specific situations or events that trigger overthinking. Are there particular contexts (e.g., social situations, work-related tasks) that lead you to spiral into negative thoughts? Identifying these triggers can help you anticipate and manage your responses in the future.

**3. Noting Emotional Responses:**

Observe how your thoughts affect your emotions. When do you feel anxious, stressed, or overwhelmed? Understanding the emotional impact of your thoughts can reveal which patterns are most detrimental to your well-being.

**4. Evaluating Decision-Making Processes:**

Analyse your decision-making habits. Do you find yourself deliberating excessively over choices? Are you prone to second-guessing your decisions long after they've been made? Recognizing these habits can help you understand how overthinking affects your ability to act.

**5. Seeking Feedback from Others:**

Sometimes, it can be challenging to recognize our own thought patterns. Seek feedback from trusted friends or family members about your thinking habits. They may provide insights into your tendencies that you might not notice yourself.

---

## The Power of Self-Awareness

Self-awareness is the foundation for recognizing and changing overthinking habits. It involves being conscious of one's thoughts, feelings, and behaviours and understanding how they influence each other.

**1. Enhancing Emotional Intelligence:**

Self-awareness enhances emotional intelligence, allowing individuals to better understand their emotions and the emotions of others. This can lead to healthier relationships and improved communication, reducing the need for overthinking.

**2. Creating a Non-Judgmental Space:**

Developing self-awareness encourages a non-judgmental approach to one's thoughts. Rather than criticising yourself for overthinking, practice observing your thoughts with curiosity and compassion. This shift in perspective can reduce the emotional weight of negative thinking.

**3. Identifying Automatic Thoughts:**

Self-awareness helps individuals identify automatic thoughts—those immediate, unfiltered responses that arise in reaction to situations. By recognizing these automatic thoughts, you can begin to challenge and reframe them, breaking the cycle of overthinking.

**4. Mindfulness Practices:**

Engaging in mindfulness practices, such as meditation or deep breathing, can enhance self-awareness. Mindfulness encourages you to observe your thoughts without judgement, helping you recognize when you are slipping into overthinking patterns.

**5. Setting Intentional Goals:**

Self-awareness allows for setting intentional goals related to thought patterns. By identifying specific habits you want to change, you can create actionable steps to reduce overthinking and foster a more balanced mindset.

## Common Cognitive Distortions

Cognitive distortions are negative thought patterns that can lead to overthinking. By identifying these distortions, individuals can challenge and reframe their thinking, reducing the intensity of their overthinking habits. Here are some of the most common cognitive distortions:

**1. All-or-Nothing Thinking:**

This distortion involves seeing situations in black-and-white terms, without recognizing any grey areas. For example, if you make a mistake at work, you might think, "I'm a complete failure." This extreme thinking prevents a balanced view of yourself and your capabilities.

**Impact on Overthinking:** All-or-nothing thinking can lead to feelings of inadequacy and fear of failure, driving individuals to overanalyze every action to avoid perceived failure.

**2. Mind Reading:**

Mind reading is the belief that you know what others are thinking, often assuming they hold negative opinions about you. For instance, you might think, "They didn't invite me to their party because they don't like me."

**Impact on Overthinking:** This distortion can lead to social anxiety and excessive worrying about how others perceive you, resulting in avoidance behaviours and ruminative thoughts about social interactions.

### 3. Catastrophizing:

This involves expecting the worst possible outcome in any situation, often without justification. For example, if you're late to a meeting, you might think, "I'll lose my job because I was late."

**Impact on Overthinking:** Catastrophizing creates a heightened sense of fear and anxiety, leading to avoidance of situations altogether and an inability to focus on constructive solutions.

### 4. Overgeneralization:

Overgeneralization involves drawing broad conclusions based on a single event. For instance, after receiving negative feedback, you might think, "I'll always mess things up."

**Impact on Overthinking:** This thought pattern can create a persistent feeling of hopelessness and encourage individuals to avoid new challenges due to fear of repeating past mistakes.

**5. Personalization:**

Personalization occurs when you take responsibility for events outside of your control. For example, if a friend is upset, you might think, "It's my fault; I must have done something wrong."

**Impact on Overthinking:** This distortion can lead to excessive guilt and self-blame, creating a cycle of overthinking that prevents individuals from seeing situations objectively.

**6. Filtering:**

Filtering involves focusing solely on the negative aspects of a situation while ignoring the positives. For instance, if you receive praise for a presentation but receive one piece of criticism, you might fixate on the criticism.

**Impact on Overthinking:** Filtering reinforces negative self-perceptions and can lead to increased anxiety about performance, driving the need to overanalyze future situations.

# Mindfulness: The Key to Mental Freedom

Mindfulness is a powerful practice that can significantly alleviate overthinking, promote mental clarity, and enhance emotional well-being. By fostering a state of awareness and presence, mindfulness allows individuals to observe their thoughts without judgement, reducing the grip of negative thought patterns.

# How Mindfulness Works to Stop Overthinking

Mindfulness works by redirecting focus and attention, allowing individuals to step back from their thoughts and emotions. This process can effectively disrupt the cycle of overthinking in several ways:

1. Awareness of Thoughts:

Mindfulness encourages individuals to become aware of their thoughts as they arise, creating a space between the thinker and the thought. This awareness helps individuals recognize overthinking patterns without getting caught up in them. By observing thoughts as transient phenomena rather than absolute truths, one can reduce their emotional impact.

2. Non-Judgmental Observation:

In mindfulness practice, individuals learn to observe their thoughts and feelings without judgement. This non-reactive stance helps to diminish feelings of guilt, shame, or frustration that often accompany overthinking. Instead of critiquing oneself for ruminating, mindfulness fosters self-compassion and acceptance.

**3. Anchoring in the Present:**

Mindfulness emphasises the importance of staying present. By focusing on the here and now, individuals can detach from spiralling thoughts about the past or future. This present-moment awareness acts as an anchor, reducing anxiety and preventing the mind from drifting into overthinking.

**4. Reducing Stress Responses:**

Mindfulness practices have been shown to activate the body's relaxation response, decreasing levels of cortisol and other stress hormones. This physiological change can help mitigate the anxiety that often drives overthinking, creating a calmer mental state.

**5. Enhancing Emotional Regulation:**

Through mindfulness, individuals develop greater emotional intelligence, enabling them to identify and understand their emotions more clearly. This understanding allows for healthier emotional responses, reducing the likelihood of becoming overwhelmed by negative feelings that fuel overthinking.

---

## Easy Mindfulness Practices for Daily Life

Incorporating mindfulness into daily routines can be simple and effective. Here are some easy practices that can help individuals cultivate mindfulness throughout their day:

**1. Mindful Breathing:**

One of the simplest forms of mindfulness practice, mindful breathing involves paying attention to your breath. Take a few moments to focus solely on the sensation of your breath entering and leaving your body. If your mind wanders, gently guide it back to your breath. This practice can be done anywhere, anytime, and is especially useful in moments of stress.

**2. Body Scan Meditation:**

A body scan involves mentally scanning your body from head to toe, noticing any sensations, tension, or areas of discomfort. This practice promotes awareness of physical sensations and encourages relaxation. Set aside 5-10 minutes to sit or lie down comfortably, and focus on each part of your body, releasing tension as you go.

**3. Mindful Walking:**

Transform a regular walk into a mindfulness practice by focusing on the sensations of walking—feeling your feet touch the ground, the rhythm of your steps, and the sights and sounds around you. Walking mindfully helps you connect with your body and the environment, enhancing your awareness of the present moment.

**4. Mindful Eating:**

Turn mealtime into a mindfulness practice by savouring each bite. Pay attention to the flavours, textures, and aromas of your food.

Eating mindfully encourages appreciation for the food and promotes healthier eating habits, while also serving as a moment of grounding in your day.

**5. Five Senses Exercise:**

Engage your senses to cultivate mindfulness. Take a moment to notice something you can see, hear, smell, taste, and touch. This practice draws your attention to the present moment and helps break the cycle of overthinking by anchoring you in your immediate environment.

---

# Grounding Techniques for Staying Present

Grounding techniques are practical strategies that help individuals reconnect with the present moment, especially during times of distress or overwhelming thoughts. Here are some effective grounding techniques to try:

**1. 5-4-3-2-1 Technique:**

This technique encourages you to ground yourself by focusing on your senses. Identify:

- **5 things you can see**
- **4 things you can touch**
- **3 things you can hear**
- **2 things you can smell**
- **1 thing you can taste**

This sensory engagement helps shift your focus away from anxious thoughts and into your immediate environment.

**2. Deep Breathing Exercises:**

Practising deep breathing can help calm your nervous system and refocus your mind. Inhale deeply through your nose for a count of four, hold your breath for a count of four, and exhale slowly through your mouth for a count of six. Repeat this cycle several times to promote relaxation and presence.

**3. Grounding Objects:**

Carry a small object, such as a smooth stone or a piece of fabric, that you can touch whenever you feel overwhelmed. Focusing on the texture and sensation of the object can help bring your attention back to the present moment.

**4. Affirmations:**

Using positive affirmations can ground you in the present. Create a list of affirmations that resonate with you, such as "I am safe in this moment" or "I have the strength to handle this." Repeat these affirmations to yourself during times of stress.

**5. Nature Connection:**

Spending time in nature can be a powerful grounding technique. Engage with your surroundings by noticing the sounds of birds, the feel of the grass beneath your feet, or the colours of the leaves. Nature has a calming effect that can help centre your thoughts.

# Controlling Your Inner Dialogue

Controlling your inner dialogue is essential for overcoming overthinking and fostering a positive mindset. Our thoughts significantly influence how we perceive ourselves and the world around us. By learning to manage this inner voice, individuals can transform their experiences, reduce anxiety, and enhance overall well-being.

## Understanding Your Inner Critic

The inner critic is that nagging voice inside your head that offers unsolicited judgments and harsh evaluations. It can manifest as self-doubt, perfectionism, or constant comparisons to others. Understanding this inner critic is the first step toward controlling your inner dialogue.

**1. Identifying the Inner Critic:**

Recognize the specific phrases and messages that your inner critic uses. Common expressions might include "You're not good enough," "You always mess things up," or "Why can't you be like them?" By identifying these negative thoughts, you can begin to see patterns in your self-talk.

**2. Origins of the Inner Critic:**

Often, the inner critic is shaped by past experiences, societal expectations, and learned behaviours. It may be rooted in childhood experiences, such as criticism from parents or peers. Understanding the origins of your inner critic can help you contextualise its presence and reduce its power.

**3. Recognizing the Impact:**

The inner critic can have a profound impact on your emotional and mental well-being. It can lead to feelings of inadequacy, anxiety, and depression, fostering a cycle of overthinking and self-sabotage. Acknowledging this impact is crucial for motivating change.

**4. Challenging the Inner Critic:**

To gain control over your inner dialogue, it's essential to challenge the inner critic's validity. Ask yourself questions like, "Is this thought based on facts?" or "Would I say this to a friend?" This critical examination can weaken the critic's authority.

---

# Reframing Negative Thoughts

Reframing involves shifting your perspective on a situation, transforming negative thoughts into more balanced and constructive ones. This technique is a powerful tool for controlling your inner dialogue and reducing overthinking.

**1. Identify Negative Thoughts:**

Begin by monitoring your thoughts and identifying negative patterns. Write down instances when you engage in negative self-talk. This practice raises awareness and helps you recognize when you are falling into a negative thought cycle.

**2. Challenge the Narrative:**

Once you've identified negative thoughts, challenge their validity. Consider evidence for and against these thoughts. For example, if you think, "I always fail," reflect on past successes and situations where you performed well.

**3. Create Alternative Perspectives:**

For each negative thought, brainstorm more balanced or positive alternatives. Instead of "I can't handle this," reframe it to "This is challenging, but I can learn and grow from it."

This shift in language can significantly affect how you perceive the situation.

**4. Practise Cognitive Distancing:**

Cognitive distancing involves viewing your thoughts as separate from yourself. Instead of saying, "I am anxious," try saying, "I am experiencing anxious thoughts." This approach can reduce the emotional weight of negative thoughts and provide clarity.

**5. Visualise Positive Outcomes:**

When faced with a negative thought, visualise a positive outcome instead. Imagine how you would feel and what steps you would take to achieve success. This technique can help rewire your brain to expect positive experiences, reducing anxiety and overthinking.

# Positive Self-Talk and Affirmations

Positive self-talk and affirmations are powerful practices that can reshape your inner dialogue, promoting a more positive and constructive mindset.

**1. The Importance of Positive Self-Talk:**

Positive self-talk involves consciously using affirming and supportive language when addressing yourself. This practice counteracts the negativity of the inner critic and fosters self-compassion and resilience.

**2. Crafting Effective Affirmations:**

Affirmations are positive statements that reinforce self-worth and capability. When creating affirmations, ensure they are specific, present-tense, and personally meaningful. For example, instead of saying, "I will be confident," use "I am confident and capable."

**3. Repetition and Consistency:**

For affirmations to be effective, they should be practised regularly. Recite your affirmations daily, ideally in front of a mirror. This repetition helps embed these positive beliefs into your subconscious, gradually transforming your inner dialogue.

**4. Incorporating Affirmations into Daily Life:**

Find moments throughout your day to incorporate affirmations. Whether during a morning routine, while commuting, or before important tasks, consistently using positive self-talk can shift your mindset and reduce overthinking.

**5. Celebrating Small Wins:**

Acknowledge and celebrate small achievements and positive qualities about yourself. This practice reinforces positive self-talk and counteracts negative narratives. For instance, after completing a task, say, "I did well on that, and I am proud of my effort."

# Cognitive Behavioral Techniques (CBT) for Overthinkers

Cognitive Behavioral Therapy (CBT) is a widely used psychological approach that focuses on the relationship between thoughts, feelings, and behaviours. For overthinkers, CBT offers practical strategies to manage and transform unhelpful thought patterns, fostering a healthier mindset and reducing anxiety.

## Challenging and Replacing Negative Thoughts

One of the core principles of CBT is the recognition that negative thoughts often distort reality, leading to unnecessary anxiety and overthinking. Learning to challenge and replace these thoughts is crucial for mental well-being.

**1. Identify Negative Thoughts:**

The first step is to become aware of the negative thoughts that contribute to overthinking. This might involve monitoring your self-talk during stressful situations. Keep a journal to note down thoughts that arise during moments of anxiety or self-doubt.

**2. Question the Validity of Thoughts:**

Once you've identified a negative thought, ask yourself a series of probing questions:

- **Is this thought based on facts or assumptions?**
- **What evidence do I have that supports or contradicts this thought?**
- **Am I overgeneralizing or jumping to conclusions?**

Challenging the validity of your thoughts helps to deconstruct their power and can lead to a more balanced perspective.

**3. Reframe Negative Thoughts:**

After questioning your thoughts, work on reframing them into more positive or realistic alternatives. For example, if you think, "I always fail," you might reframe it as, "I have faced challenges before, and I have learned from them." This reframing process can shift your emotional response and reduce the grip of negative thinking.

**4. Create a Positive Thought Replacement:**

Develop a list of positive affirmations or statements that you can use to replace negative thoughts. When a negative thought arises, consciously replace it with a pre-prepared positive statement. For instance, when faced with self-doubt, remind yourself, "I am capable, and I can handle this situation."

## Thought Records and Journaling

Thought records and journaling are valuable CBT tools that help individuals track and analyse their thoughts, providing insight into patterns of overthinking.

**1. Understanding Thought Records:**

A thought record is a structured way to document negative thoughts and the circumstances surrounding them. It typically includes sections for:

- **Situation:** Describe the event that triggered the thought.
- **Thoughts:** Write down the automatic negative thoughts that arose.
- **Emotions:** Identify the feelings associated with those thoughts.
- **Evidence:** List evidence that supports and contradicts the thought.
- **Alternative Thoughts:** Develop more balanced or realistic alternatives.

This structured approach allows you to gain clarity and distance from your thoughts, making it easier to challenge and replace them.

**2. Journaling for Self-Reflection:**

Journaling can serve as a powerful reflective tool. Set aside time each day to write about your thoughts and feelings. Focus on moments of overthinking and describe how they affected your mood and behaviour. Reflecting on these experiences helps you identify patterns and triggers, which can inform your coping strategies.

**3. Daily Gratitude Journals:**

Incorporating a gratitude journal into your routine can shift your focus from negative thinking to positive experiences. Each day, write down three things you are grateful for, which can help counterbalance the negative thoughts associated with overthinking.

**4. Progress Tracking:**

Regularly review your thought records and journal entries to track your progress. Celebrate moments of growth and recognize when you successfully challenged negative thoughts or engaged in positive self-talk.

# Behavioural Experiments: Testing Your Thoughts

Behavioural experiments are practical activities that allow individuals to test the validity of their thoughts in real-life situations. This technique helps bridge the gap between thought and action, fostering experiential learning.

**1. Design Your Experiment:**

Identify a specific thought or belief you want to test. For example, if you often think, "If I speak up in a meeting, everyone will judge me," design an experiment to challenge this belief. Set a goal to share an idea during the next meeting.

**2. Outline the Hypothesis:**

Before conducting the experiment, outline your hypothesis. What do you believe will happen if you engage in this behaviour? Write down your expected outcomes and how you anticipate you will feel.

**3. Conduct the Experiment:**

Take action based on your hypothesis. Engage in the behaviour you've outlined, whether it's speaking up in a meeting, reaching out to a friend, or trying something new. Be mindful of your thoughts and feelings during the experience.

**4. Analyse the Results:**

After the experiment, reflect on the outcomes. Did the experience align with your initial thoughts? Were the results as negative as you anticipated? This analysis can provide valuable insights into the irrationality of some fears and help diminish their power.

**5. Adjust Future Thoughts:**

Based on your findings, adjust your beliefs and thoughts accordingly. If the results of your experiment contradict your initial negative beliefs, remind yourself of this evidence in future situations. This reinforcement helps create a new, more positive narrative.

# Stress and Anxiety Management

Managing stress and anxiety is crucial for overthinkers, as these conditions can exacerbate negative thought patterns and hinder emotional well-being. By understanding the relationship between stress and overthinking, employing relaxation techniques, and developing healthy coping mechanisms, individuals can cultivate resilience and improve their mental health.

## How Stress Fuels Overthinking

Stress is a natural response to perceived threats or challenges, triggering the body's fight-or-flight response. However, when stress becomes chronic or overwhelming, it can significantly impact mental health, leading to overthinking. Here are several ways stress contributes to this cycle:

**1. Heightened Sensitivity to Stressors:**

When under stress, individuals may become more sensitive to external triggers. Everyday situations, such as a deadline at work or a disagreement with a friend, can amplify feelings of anxiety, leading to excessive rumination.

**2. Cognitive Load:**

Stress increases cognitive load, making it more challenging to process thoughts and emotions clearly. Overthinkers may find themselves trapped in a cycle of negative thinking, where stress clouds their judgement and inhibits rational decision-making.

**3. Negative Thought Patterns:**

Chronic stress can reinforce negative thought patterns, such as catastrophizing or all-or-nothing thinking. This mindset can make individuals feel as though they have little control over their circumstances, further fueling anxiety and overthinking.

**4. Impaired Emotional Regulation:**

Stress can impair emotional regulation, making it difficult for individuals to manage their feelings effectively. This emotional dysregulation can lead to heightened anxiety and an inability to break free from negative thought spirals.

**5. Physical Symptoms of Stress:**

Stress often manifests physically, leading to symptoms such as fatigue, tension, and insomnia. These physical symptoms can exacerbate anxiety and overthinking, creating a vicious cycle that becomes increasingly difficult to escape.

## Relaxation Techniques: Breathing, Meditation, and Visualization

Incorporating relaxation techniques into daily routines can significantly reduce stress and anxiety, helping to mitigate overthinking. Here are three effective techniques:

**1. Breathing Exercises:**

Breathing exercises are a simple yet powerful way to induce relaxation and calm the mind. They can be practised anywhere and take only a few minutes.

- **Deep Breathing:** Sit or lie down comfortably. Inhale deeply through your nose for a count of four, allowing your abdomen to expand. Hold your breath for a count of four, then exhale slowly through your mouth for a count of six. Repeat this cycle several times, focusing on the rhythm of your breath.
- **4-7-8 Breathing:** Inhale through your nose for a count of four, hold your breath

for a count of seven, and exhale through your mouth for a count of eight. This technique can help reduce anxiety and promote relaxation.

**2. Meditation:**

Meditation is a mindfulness practice that encourages present-moment awareness and can effectively reduce stress and overthinking.

- **Guided Meditation:** Use a meditation app or online resource to find guided meditations focused on relaxation and stress relief. These sessions typically include instructions for focusing on your breath or visualising peaceful scenes.
- **Mindfulness Meditation:** Sit in a comfortable position and focus your attention on your breath. If your mind begins to wander, gently redirect your focus back to your breathing. Start with a few minutes each day and gradually increase the duration as you become more comfortable with the practice.

### 3. Visualisation:

Visualisation involves creating mental images of calming and peaceful scenarios, which can help reduce stress and anxiety.

- **Calm Place Visualisation:** Close your eyes and imagine a place where you feel safe and relaxed, such as a beach, forest, or favourite room. Engage all your senses by imagining the sights, sounds, smells, and textures of this place. Spend a few minutes immersed in this visualisation, allowing the calmness of the scene to wash over you.
- **Future Success Visualisation:** Picture a future scenario where you handle a challenging situation successfully. Visualise yourself managing your emotions and responding positively. This technique can boost confidence and reduce anxiety about future events.

## Developing Healthy Coping Mechanisms

Developing healthy coping mechanisms is essential for managing stress and anxiety effectively. By cultivating positive strategies, individuals can better navigate challenges without succumbing to overthinking.

**1. Physical Activity:**

Regular physical activity is one of the most effective ways to reduce stress and improve mental health. Exercise releases endorphins, which act as natural mood lifters.

- **Incorporate Movement:** Aim for at least 30 minutes of moderate exercise most days of the week. This could include walking, running, dancing, or participating in a group sport. Choose activities that you enjoy to make it sustainable.

**2. Healthy Lifestyle Choices:**

Adopting a healthy lifestyle can positively impact stress levels and mental well-being.

- **Nutrition:** Eating a balanced diet rich in whole foods, fruits, vegetables, lean proteins, and healthy fats can provide the nutrients your body needs to cope with stress. Avoid excessive caffeine and sugar, which can contribute to anxiety.
- **Sleep Hygiene:** Prioritise sleep by establishing a consistent sleep schedule, creating a relaxing bedtime routine, and ensuring your sleep environment is comfortable and conducive to rest.

3. Social Support:

Building a strong support network is vital for managing stress and anxiety. Connecting with friends, family, or support groups can provide encouragement and perspective.

- **Talk About Your Feelings:** Share your thoughts and feelings with trusted individuals. Talking about your

experiences can help you process emotions and gain insights from others.
- **Engage in Social Activities:** Participate in social events or group activities that you enjoy. Building connections with others can provide a sense of belonging and reduce feelings of isolation.

**4. Time Management and Organization:**

Effective time management can alleviate feelings of being overwhelmed, a common trigger for overthinking.

- **Prioritise Tasks:** Make a list of tasks and prioritise them based on importance and deadlines. Break large tasks into smaller, manageable steps to avoid feeling overwhelmed.
- **Set Boundaries:** Learn to say no to additional commitments when you're already feeling stressed. Setting boundaries is essential for protecting your time and mental health.

**5. Creative Outlets:**

Engaging in creative activities can provide an emotional release and serve as a distraction from overthinking.

- **Art and Crafting:** Explore painting, drawing, knitting, or other crafts that allow for creative expression. These activities can be therapeutic and help reduce stress.
- **Writing and Journaling:** Writing about your thoughts and feelings can provide clarity and emotional relief. Consider keeping a journal where you express your experiences, thoughts, and reflections.

# The Power of Decision-Making

Decision-making is a fundamental skill that influences every aspect of our lives, from personal choices to professional paths. For overthinkers, the act of making decisions can often feel overwhelming, leading to anxiety and indecision. Understanding the power of decision-making, employing effective strategies, setting healthy boundaries, and overcoming the quest for perfection can significantly enhance one's ability to make confident choices.

---

# Strategies to Make Decisions with Confidence

Making decisions with confidence involves adopting effective strategies that simplify the process and reduce the emotional burden. Here are several techniques to help you navigate decision-making more effectively:

**1. Clarify Your Goals:**

Before making a decision, it's essential to clarify your goals and values. Consider what is most important to you in the situation at hand. Ask yourself:

- What outcome am I hoping to achieve?
- How does this decision align with my values and long-term goals?

Having a clear understanding of your objectives provides a framework for making choices that resonate with your true self.

**2. Gather Relevant Information:**

**Overthinker's Bible**

While overthinking often leads to excessive information gathering, it's crucial to strike a balance. Focus on collecting relevant information that will aid your decision-making process without becoming overwhelmed.

- Identify key facts or data points that directly impact your decision.
- Limit your research to reputable sources to avoid information overload.

**3. Set a Time Limit:**

To combat indecision, set a specific time limit for making your decision. This approach prevents prolonged deliberation and encourages prompt action.

- Determine a realistic timeframe based on the complexity of the decision.
- Stick to this timeline to help foster accountability and prompt resolution.

**4. Use a Decision-Making Framework:**

Employing a structured decision-making framework can help streamline the process. Here are a couple of popular methods:

- **Pros and Cons List:** Create a list of advantages and disadvantages for each option. This visual representation can help clarify your thoughts and make the consequences of each choice more tangible.
- **Weighted Decision Matrix:** For more complex decisions, create a matrix to evaluate options against criteria important to you. Assign weights to each criterion based on its significance, then score each option accordingly to identify the best choice.

**5. Trust Your Instincts:**

Intuition plays a vital role in decision-making. While rational analysis is important, don't underestimate the value of gut feelings.

- Pay attention to your emotional responses when considering different options.

Sometimes, your instincts can guide you toward the right choice, even when the logical analysis feels uncertain.

**6. Accept Imperfection:**

Recognize that no decision is perfect, and that uncertainty is a natural part of life. Accepting that you may not have all the answers can relieve the pressure of needing to make the "perfect" choice.

---

# Setting Boundaries with Yourself

Setting boundaries with yourself is essential for effective decision-making and can help mitigate the negative impacts of overthinking. Here are strategies to establish these boundaries:

**1. Define Decision-Making Parameters:**

Establish specific parameters for how you will approach decision-making. This could involve determining which types of decisions require extensive analysis and which can be made more intuitively.

- For routine or minor decisions, allow yourself to decide quickly without excessive deliberation.
- Reserve more time and analysis for significant or life-altering choices.

**2. Limit Information Sources:**

To prevent information overload, limit the number of sources you consult when gathering information for a decision.

- Identify a few trusted resources that provide the necessary insights without overwhelming you with excessive data.
- This helps to streamline the decision-making process and maintain focus.

**3. Practice Saying No:**

Part of setting boundaries involves learning to say no to additional commitments or obligations that may complicate your decision-making process.

- Assess your current commitments and evaluate whether they align with your priorities.
- Be willing to decline new opportunities if they detract from your focus on existing goals.

**4. Create a Decision-Making Routine:**

Establish a routine or ritual for decision-making that helps signal your mind and body that it's time to focus.

- This could include a quiet moment of reflection, a short meditation, or a specific environment conducive to thoughtful decision-making.
- A consistent routine can help ground you and enhance your confidence during the decision-making process.

# How to Stop Seeking Perfection

The pursuit of perfection can paralyse decision-making and contribute to overthinking. Learning to embrace imperfection is crucial for making confident choices. Here are strategies to help you move away from perfectionism:

**1. Reframe Your Perspective:**

Shift your mindset from seeking perfection to striving for progress.

- Understand that perfection is often unattainable, and that aiming for progress allows for growth and learning.
- Remind yourself that mistakes and failures are valuable opportunities for improvement.

**2. Set Realistic Standards:**

Establish realistic standards for yourself rather than unattainable ideals.

- Recognize that excellence does not require perfection; aim for doing your best within reasonable parameters.
- Celebrate small achievements and incremental progress, which can motivate you to continue moving forward.

**3. Embrace a Growth Mindset:**

Adopt a growth mindset, which emphasises the belief that abilities and intelligence can be developed through dedication and effort.

- View challenges and setbacks as opportunities for learning rather than as reflections of your worth or capability.
- This mindset encourages resilience and a willingness to take risks, ultimately enhancing your decision-making confidence.

**4. Limit Comparison to Others:**

Comparison to others often fuels the desire for perfection. Focus on your own journey and progress instead.

- Avoid dwelling on how others are performing; instead, focus on your own growth and achievements.
- Surround yourself with supportive individuals who encourage your journey without fostering a competitive atmosphere.

**5. Practice Self-Compassion:**

Cultivate self-compassion by treating yourself with kindness and understanding, especially in moments of difficulty or decision-making.

- Acknowledge that everyone makes mistakes and faces challenges; allow yourself to be human.
- Practising self-compassion can reduce anxiety and foster a more positive relationship with your decision-making process.

# Building Mental Resilience

Mental resilience refers to the ability to adapt to challenges, recover from setbacks, and maintain a positive outlook in the face of adversity. Building mental resilience is crucial for navigating life's inevitable ups and downs, enhancing emotional well-being, and promoting personal growth.

---

## How to Handle Uncertainty

Uncertainty is an unavoidable part of life that can lead to anxiety and overthinking. Learning to handle uncertainty effectively is essential for developing resilience. Here are several strategies to help manage uncertainty:

**1. Embrace the Unknown:**

Accepting that uncertainty is a natural aspect of life can reduce the anxiety associated with it.

- **Shift Your Mindset:** Instead of fearing the unknown, view it as an opportunity for growth and exploration. Recognize that uncertainty can lead to new experiences and learning.
- **Focus on What You Can Control:** Identify aspects of your situation that you can influence and take proactive steps. This focus can provide a sense of agency and reduce feelings of helplessness.

**2. Practice Mindfulness:**

Mindfulness techniques can help ground you in the present moment, reducing anxiety about future uncertainties.

- **Breathing Exercises:** Engage in deep breathing or guided meditations to calm

your mind and body. This practice helps create a sense of peace and reduces the tendency to overthink.
- **Body Scan:** Conduct a body scan meditation, focusing your awareness on different parts of your body. This technique fosters awareness and encourages relaxation, allowing you to accept uncertainty without excessive worry.

**3. Limit Information Overload:**

In the age of information, it's easy to become overwhelmed by the constant flow of news and updates.

- **Set Boundaries for Information Consumption:** Designate specific times for checking news or social media. Limit exposure to sources that increase your anxiety, focusing instead on information that is relevant and constructive.
- **Seek Reliable Sources:** When looking for information, stick to credible sources.

Avoid sensationalised news, which can amplify uncertainty and fear.

### 4. Develop Contingency Plans:

While you can't predict the future, having contingency plans can provide a sense of preparedness and reduce anxiety.

- **Identify Possible Scenarios:** Think through potential challenges you might face and outline how you would respond. This proactive approach can help you feel more equipped to handle uncertainty.
- **Flexibility is Key:** While planning is essential, remain open to adjusting your plans as circumstances evolve. Flexibility fosters adaptability and resilience.

### 5. Connect with Support Networks:

Reach out to friends, family, or support groups when dealing with uncertainty. Sharing your concerns can provide perspective and reassurance.

- **Open Conversations:** Discuss your feelings of uncertainty with trusted individuals. Talking about your fears can help normalise them and reduce feelings of isolation.
- **Seek Professional Help:** If uncertainty becomes overwhelming, consider speaking with a mental health professional. Therapy can provide tools for coping with anxiety and uncertainty more effectively.

## Cultivating Optimism and a Growth Mindset

Optimism and a growth mindset are powerful attributes that contribute to mental resilience. They enable individuals to view challenges as opportunities and maintain a positive outlook, even during difficult times.

**1. Practice Gratitude:**

Gratitude is a key component of optimism. Regularly reflecting on what you are thankful for can shift your focus from negativity to positivity.

- **Daily Gratitude Journaling:** Keep a gratitude journal where you write down three things you are grateful for each day. This practice encourages a positive mindset and helps you appreciate the good in your life.
- **Express Gratitude to Others:** Take the time to express appreciation to those around you. Acknowledging the support and kindness of others fosters positive relationships and strengthens your sense of community.

2. Reframe Challenges:

Reframing challenges as opportunities for growth is essential for cultivating a growth mindset.

- **View Setbacks as Learning Experiences:** Instead of seeing failures as final, approach them as opportunities to

learn and improve. Ask yourself what lessons can be drawn from the situation.
- **Focus on Effort Over Outcome:** Emphasise the importance of effort and persistence rather than solely the results. Celebrate your hard work and resilience, regardless of the outcome.

**3. Surround Yourself with Positivity:**

The people and environments you engage with can significantly influence your mindset.

- **Seek Positive Influences:** Surround yourself with individuals who uplift and inspire you. Engage in discussions that encourage growth and positivity.
- **Create a Positive Environment:** Curate your physical and emotional environment to support your mental well-being. This could include decluttering your space, displaying positive affirmations, or engaging in activities that bring you joy.

**4. Embrace Lifelong Learning:**

A growth mindset thrives on curiosity and a willingness to learn.

- **Challenge Yourself:** Step outside your comfort zone by trying new activities, pursuing new interests, or taking on challenges. Embracing discomfort can lead to personal growth and increased resilience.
- **Seek Feedback:** Be open to feedback from others and use it as a tool for improvement. Constructive criticism can help you develop new skills and enhance your self-awareness.

## Strengthening Emotional Intelligence

Emotional intelligence (EI) is the ability to recognize, understand, and manage our emotions and the emotions of others. Strengthening EI is essential for building resilience and navigating relationships effectively.

### 1. Enhance Self-Awareness:

Self-awareness is the foundation of emotional intelligence. Being aware of your emotions allows you to respond thoughtfully rather than react impulsively.

- **Regular Reflection:** Take time to reflect on your emotional responses throughout the day. Consider journaling your thoughts and feelings to gain insight into your emotional patterns.
- **Mindfulness Practices:** Engage in mindfulness techniques to develop a deeper awareness of your emotions in real time. This practice can help you recognize emotional triggers and respond more effectively.

### 2. Manage Emotions:

Learning to regulate your emotions is crucial for maintaining resilience.

- **Develop Coping Strategies:** Identify healthy coping mechanisms to manage

overwhelming emotions. This may include deep breathing, engaging in physical activity, or seeking social support.
- **Pause Before Reacting:** When faced with strong emotions, take a moment to pause and assess your feelings before reacting. This mindfulness practice can help you respond thoughtfully rather than impulsively.

### 3. Improve Empathy:

Empathy, the ability to understand and share the feelings of others, is a vital aspect of emotional intelligence.

- **Practise Active Listening:** Engage in active listening by fully focusing on the speaker without interrupting. Reflect back what you've heard to ensure understanding and demonstrate empathy.
- **Put Yourself in Others' Shoes:** Try to view situations from the perspectives of others. Consider how they might be

feeling and the challenges they face, which can enhance your understanding and strengthen relationships.

**4. Build Strong Relationships:**

Strong relationships are a key component of resilience. Nurturing positive connections with others can provide support during challenging times.

- **Invest Time in Relationships:** Make a conscious effort to strengthen your connections with family, friends, and colleagues. Engage in meaningful conversations and shared activities to foster deeper bonds.
- **Communicate Openly:** Practise open and honest communication in your relationships. Share your thoughts and feelings while encouraging others to do the same. This transparency can build trust and understanding.

# Developing Focus and Clarity

In our fast-paced, information-saturated world, developing focus and clarity is essential for mental well-being and effective decision-making. The ability to prioritise what truly matters, manage time effectively, and practise the art of letting go can significantly enhance one's focus and clarity.

## How to Prioritise What Really Matters

Prioritisation is a skill that enables individuals to focus on what truly matters, reducing overwhelm and increasing productivity. Here are some effective strategies for prioritising your tasks and commitments:

**1. Identify Your Core Values:**

Understanding your core values is fundamental to prioritising effectively.

- **Reflect on What Matters Most:** Take time to identify your personal values, such as family, health, career, or creativity. Consider how these values influence your decisions and priorities.
- **Align Tasks with Values:** When faced with tasks or commitments, evaluate how they align with your core values. This alignment helps clarify what deserves your attention and effort.

**2. Use the Eisenhower Matrix:**

The Eisenhower Matrix is a simple tool for prioritisation that categorises tasks based on urgency and importance.

- **Quadrant 1:** Urgent and Important – Do these tasks immediately.
- **Quadrant 2:** Important but Not Urgent – Schedule these tasks to complete them later.
- **Quadrant 3:** Urgent but Not Important – Delegate these tasks if possible.
- **Quadrant 4:** Not Urgent and Not Important – Eliminate or minimise these tasks.

Using this framework can help you focus on tasks that have the most significant impact on your goals.

### 3. Set SMART Goals:

Setting SMART goals—Specific, Measurable, Achievable, Relevant, and Time-bound—can guide your prioritisation process.

- **Specific:** Clearly define what you want to achieve.
- **Measurable:** Identify how you will measure success.
- **Achievable:** Ensure your goals are realistic and attainable.
- **Relevant:** Align your goals with your values and long-term vision.
- **Time-bound:** Set a deadline to create a sense of urgency.

SMART goals provide clarity and direction, helping you prioritise effectively.

**4. Break Tasks into Smaller Steps:**

Large tasks can feel overwhelming, leading to procrastination. Breaking tasks into smaller, manageable steps can help you prioritise and make progress.

- **Create Actionable Steps:** For each task, outline specific steps needed to complete it. This breakdown simplifies the process and makes it easier to start.

- **Tackle One Step at a Time:** Focus on completing one small step at a time, which can boost motivation and prevent overwhelm.

**5. Regularly Review and Adjust Priorities:**

Priorities can shift over time based on circumstances and new information. Regularly reviewing and adjusting your priorities is crucial.

- **Schedule Time for Reflection:** Set aside time each week or month to assess your current priorities. Reflect on what's working and what isn't.
- **Be Flexible:** Be willing to adjust your priorities as necessary. Life is dynamic, and flexibility allows you to respond effectively to changes.

---

# Time Management for a Clearer Mind

Effective time management is key to developing focus and clarity. By managing your time wisely, you can reduce stress and create a more organised approach to your tasks.

**1. Create a Daily Schedule:**

Establishing a daily schedule can help you structure your time effectively.

- **Block Time for Tasks:** Allocate specific blocks of time for different tasks, ensuring you dedicate time to your highest priorities. Use tools like calendars or planners to visualise your schedule.
- **Include Breaks:** Don't forget to schedule breaks. Short breaks can improve focus and prevent burnout.

**2. Use Time Management Techniques:**

Several techniques can enhance your time management skills:

- **Pomodoro Technique:** Work in focused intervals (usually 25 minutes) followed by a 5-minute break. After four intervals,

take a longer break (15-30 minutes). This method can enhance focus and productivity.
- **Time Blocking:** Allocate specific time blocks for different categories of tasks (e.g., work, exercise, family time). This method can help you maintain balance and ensure all areas of your life receive attention.

### 3. Limit Distractions:

Identifying and minimising distractions is essential for effective time management.

- **Create a Distraction-Free Workspace:** Designate a workspace that is free from distractions. Keep your environment organised and limit access to distracting devices or websites.
- **Turn Off Notifications:** Disable notifications on your phone and computer while working to maintain focus. Set specific times to check messages and emails to avoid constant interruptions.

### 4. Learn to Say No:

Understanding your limits and being willing to say no to additional commitments can help protect your time.

- **Evaluate Requests:** When faced with new commitments, assess how they align with your priorities. If they don't add value or align with your goals, it's okay to decline.
- **Be Assertive:** Practise assertiveness in communicating your boundaries. Politely decline requests that interfere with your focus and priorities.

### 5. Reflect on Time Usage:

Regularly reflecting on how you spend your time can help identify areas for improvement.

- **Track Your Time:** Use a time-tracking app or journal to log your daily activities. Analysing how you spend your time can reveal patterns and areas for adjustment.

- **Adjust as Needed:** Based on your reflection, make necessary adjustments to your schedule and habits. Continuous improvement will enhance your time management skills.

## The Art of Letting Go

Letting go of unnecessary burdens, negative thoughts, and unproductive habits is a vital component of developing focus and clarity. Learning to release what no longer serves you can create space for positive growth.

### 1. Identify What to Let Go:

Recognizing what to release is the first step in the process.

- **Reflect on Your Life:** Take time to consider areas of your life where you feel burdened or stuck. Identify specific thoughts, habits, or commitments that weigh you down.

- **Consider the Impact:** Evaluate how these burdens impact your mental clarity and overall well-being. If something doesn't contribute positively, it may be time to let it go.

2. Practice Acceptance:

Acceptance is a powerful tool for letting go.

- **Acknowledge Your Feelings:** Allow yourself to feel emotions associated with letting go. Acknowledging your feelings can help you process them more effectively.
- **Practice Self-Compassion:** Be kind to yourself during this process. Understand that letting go can be challenging, and it's okay to experience a range of emotions.

3. Use Mindfulness Techniques:

Mindfulness can help facilitate the letting-go process.

- **Meditation:** Engage in meditation focused on releasing thoughts or feelings

that no longer serve you. Visualise letting go of burdens with each exhale.
- **Journaling:** Write down your thoughts and feelings about what you wish to release. This practice can provide clarity and serve as a symbolic gesture of letting go.

#### 4. Replace Negative Habits with Positive Ones:

To truly let go, replace negative habits with positive alternatives.

- **Identify Replacement Habits:** Determine positive habits that can take the place of what you're letting go. For example, if you're releasing procrastination, commit to a focused work routine.
- **Create a Plan:** Develop a plan for implementing new habits. Setting small, achievable goals can help you gradually transition away from old patterns.

#### 5. Celebrate Your Progress:

Acknowledging your progress is essential for reinforcing the letting-go process.

- **Reflect on Achievements:** Take time to reflect on the positive changes you've made. Celebrate your successes, no matter how small, as they contribute to your growth.
- **Maintain a Positive Mindset:** Focus on the benefits of letting go, such as increased clarity, reduced stress, and enhanced focus. A positive mindset can motivate you to continue on your journey.

# Finding Peace in the Present

In a world filled with distractions and uncertainties, finding peace in the present moment is crucial for mental clarity and emotional well-being. Cultivating mindfulness, practising gratitude, learning to surrender control, and living with purpose can help individuals navigate their thoughts and emotions more effectively. This section explores these transformative practices in depth.

## Gratitude Practices to Calm Your Mind

Gratitude is a powerful practice that can shift your focus from negative thoughts to positive experiences, fostering a sense of peace and contentment. Here are several effective gratitude practices to help calm your mind:

**1. Daily Gratitude Journaling:**

Keeping a gratitude journal is an excellent way to cultivate appreciation and mindfulness.

- **Set Aside Time:** Dedicate a few minutes each day to write down three to five things you are grateful for. These can be big or small, from a supportive friend to a beautiful sunset.
- **Reflect on Your Entries:** Spend time reflecting on why you are grateful for these things. This reflection deepens your appreciation and encourages a positive mindset.

**2. Gratitude Meditation:**

Incorporating gratitude into meditation can enhance mindfulness and promote inner peace.

- **Guided Gratitude Meditation:** Find a guided meditation focused on gratitude. Many apps and online resources offer sessions that lead you through reflecting on the things you appreciate.
- **Silent Meditation:** Sit in silence and focus on your breath. With each inhale, think of something you are grateful for, and with each exhale, release any tension or negativity.

3. Express Gratitude to Others:

Sharing your appreciation with others strengthens relationships and fosters a sense of community.

- **Write Thank-You Notes:** Take time to write heartfelt notes to friends, family, or colleagues expressing your gratitude for their support or kindness.
- **Verbal Acknowledgment:** Make a habit of expressing thanks in conversations. A simple "thank you" can create positive connections and uplift both parties.

### 4. Create a Gratitude Jar:

A gratitude jar is a fun and visual way to practise gratitude.

- **Materials Needed:** Find a jar and some small pieces of paper.
- **Weekly Reflection:** Each week, write down one thing you are grateful for and place it in the jar. At the end of the month or year, review the notes to remind yourself of the positive moments in your life.

### 5. Gratitude Walks:

Combine physical activity with gratitude for a powerful experience.

- **Mindful Walking:** Go for a walk and intentionally observe your surroundings. As you walk, think of things you are grateful for related to your environment, such as the beauty of nature or the warmth of the sun.

- **Engage Your Senses:** Pay attention to the sights, sounds, and smells around you. Engaging your senses can enhance your sense of presence and appreciation for the moment.

---

# How to Surrender Control and Embrace the Unknown

Surrendering control can be challenging, especially for overthinkers who thrive on predictability. However, learning to embrace uncertainty can lead to greater peace and acceptance. Here are strategies to help you surrender control:

**1. Acknowledge Your Need for Control:**

Understanding your desire for control is the first step toward letting go.

- **Self-Reflection:** Take time to reflect on situations where you feel the need to

control outcomes. Consider how this need impacts your well-being and relationships.
- **Recognize Limitations:** Accept that not everything is within your control. Embracing this reality can reduce anxiety and open you up to new possibilities.

**2. Practice Mindfulness:**

Mindfulness helps you stay grounded in the present and reduces the urge to control future outcomes.

- **Focus on the Here and Now:** Engage in mindfulness practices such as meditation, deep breathing, or body scans to centre yourself in the present moment.
- **Let Thoughts Come and Go:** When anxious thoughts about the future arise, acknowledge them without judgement and let them pass. This practice helps create space for acceptance.

**3. Reframe Your Perspective:**

Changing your perspective on uncertainty can ease the burden of control.

- **View Uncertainty as Opportunity:** Instead of fearing the unknown, see it as a chance for growth and new experiences. This shift in mindset can make uncertainty feel less daunting.
- **Practice Acceptance:** Accept that uncertainty is a natural part of life. Embrace the idea that life unfolds in unexpected ways, and that's okay.

4. Set Intentions Instead of Expectations:

Setting intentions can guide your actions without the pressure of rigid expectations.

- **Focus on Values and Goals:** Rather than fixating on specific outcomes, set intentions based on your values and what you hope to achieve. This approach fosters flexibility and adaptability.
- **Stay Open to Possibilities:** Allow yourself to explore different paths rather than adhering strictly to a predetermined

plan. This openness can lead to unexpected opportunities.

**5. Seek Support:**

Embracing uncertainty can be easier with support from others.

- **Share Your Feelings:** Talk about your feelings of uncertainty with trusted friends or family members. Sharing your thoughts can provide perspective and reassurance.
- **Consider Professional Guidance:** If surrendering control feels particularly challenging, consider seeking support from a therapist or counsellor. They can provide tools and strategies to help you navigate uncertainty.

---

# Living a Life of Purpose Beyond Overthinking

Finding and living a life of purpose can provide direction and meaning, reducing the tendency to overthink. Here are ways to discover and embrace your purpose:

1. Explore Your Passions:

Identifying what you are passionate about can guide you toward a purposeful life.

- **Reflect on Interests:** Take time to reflect on activities that bring you joy and fulfilment. Consider hobbies, subjects, or causes that resonate with you deeply.
- **Engage in New Experiences:** Try new activities or volunteer for causes that interest you. Exploring diverse experiences can help you uncover hidden passions.

2. Define Your Values:

Understanding your core values is essential for living purposefully.

- **Identify Core Values:** Make a list of values that are important to you, such as integrity, compassion, creativity, or community.

- **Align Actions with Values:** Assess how your current actions and goals align with your values. Strive to engage in activities that reflect what matters most to you.

**3. Set Meaningful Goals:**

Establishing goals that align with your passions and values can provide direction and motivation.

- **Create SMART Goals:** Use the SMART framework (Specific, Measurable, Achievable, Relevant, Time-bound) to set goals that resonate with your sense of purpose.
- **Break Goals into Steps:** Break your goals into manageable steps to create a sense of progress and achievement. Celebrate small victories along the way.

**4. Cultivate a Growth Mindset:**

Embracing a growth mindset fosters resilience and adaptability, essential for living a purposeful life.

- **Embrace Challenges:** View challenges as opportunities for growth rather than obstacles. This mindset can empower you to push through difficulties and learn from experiences.
- **Stay Curious:** Cultivate curiosity and a willingness to learn. Seek knowledge and experiences that expand your understanding of yourself and the world around you.

5. Practice Self-Compassion:

Being kind to yourself is crucial when navigating purpose and overthinking.

- **Acknowledge Your Journey:** Recognize that finding purpose is a journey that may take time. Be patient with yourself as you explore and grow.
- **Let Go of Perfectionism:** Understand that there is no perfect path to purpose. Embrace imperfections and allow yourself to learn and evolve.

# Sustaining Mental Clarity

Maintaining mental clarity is essential for making sound decisions, fostering creativity, and enhancing overall well-being. It involves cultivating habits that support a clear mind, establishing routines that prioritise mental wellness, and recognizing the critical roles of sleep, nutrition, and exercise.

---

## Daily Habits for a Clear Mind

Developing daily habits can significantly enhance your mental clarity and overall cognitive function. Here are several effective habits to incorporate into your daily life:

**1. Mindful Mornings:**

Starting your day with mindfulness sets a positive tone for mental clarity.

- **Meditation or Deep Breathing:** Begin your day with a few minutes of meditation or deep breathing exercises. This practice calms the mind and prepares you for the day ahead.
- **Gratitude Practice:** Spend a few moments reflecting on what you're grateful for. This positive mindset helps to focus your thoughts and reduce stress.

**2. Prioritising Tasks:**

A clear mind is often linked to effective time management.

- **Daily Planning:** Each morning, list your tasks for the day. Prioritise them based on urgency and importance to maintain focus on what truly matters.

- **Time Blocking:** Use time-blocking techniques to allocate specific periods for tasks. This helps prevent multitasking and minimises distractions.

**3. Digital Detox:**

Reducing digital distractions can greatly enhance mental clarity.

- **Limit Screen Time:** Set specific times for checking emails and social media to avoid constant interruptions. Consider "screen-free" hours to give your mind a break.
- **Focus on One Task:** Practise single-tasking rather than multitasking. Concentrating on one task at a time enhances productivity and clarity.

**4. Breaks and Downtime:**

Regular breaks are crucial for sustaining mental clarity.

- **Pomodoro Technique:** Use the Pomodoro Technique, where you work for 25

minutes and then take a 5-minute break. This structure keeps your mind fresh and focused.
- **Nature Breaks:** Spend time outdoors during breaks. Nature has a calming effect and can help reset your mind, providing clarity and inspiration.

---

# Building a Routine for Mental Wellness

A well-structured routine is fundamental for maintaining mental clarity and overall wellness. Here's how to build an effective routine:

**1. Establish a Consistent Wake-Up and Sleep Schedule:**

Consistency in sleep patterns is vital for mental clarity.

- **Set Regular Sleep Times:** Aim for 7-9 hours of quality sleep each night by going to bed and waking up at the same time

daily. Consistent sleep supports cognitive function and emotional regulation.
- **Create a Relaxing Bedtime Ritual:** Establish a calming pre-sleep routine, such as reading or gentle stretching, to signal to your body that it's time to wind down.

**2. Incorporate Physical Activity:**

Exercise plays a significant role in mental clarity.

- **Daily Movement:** Aim for at least 30 minutes of moderate exercise each day. This could be walking, jogging, yoga, or any activity you enjoy. Exercise boosts endorphins, enhancing mood and clarity.
- **Stretching and Mobility Work:** Incorporate stretching or yoga into your routine. These practices help release tension, improve focus, and promote relaxation.

**3. Schedule Time for Reflection:**

Reflection allows you to process your thoughts and feelings.

- **End-of-Day Journaling:** Spend a few minutes each evening journaling about your day. Reflect on what went well and what could be improved. This practice helps clarify your thoughts and feelings.
- **Mindfulness Reflection:** Incorporate mindfulness into your evening routine. Spend a few moments reflecting on your day, focusing on your emotions and experiences without judgement.

4. Designate "Me Time":

Allocating time for self-care is essential for mental clarity.

- **Engage in Hobbies:** Dedicate time each week to engage in activities that bring you joy, such as reading, painting, or gardening. Hobbies provide an outlet for creativity and relaxation.
- **Social Connections:** Make time for meaningful social interactions.

Connecting with friends and loved ones can enhance your sense of belonging and reduce feelings of isolation.

---

## The Role of Sleep, Nutrition, and Exercise

Sustaining mental clarity heavily relies on three critical components: sleep, nutrition, and exercise. Here's how each contributes to mental wellness:

**1. Sleep: The Foundation of Mental Clarity**

Quality sleep is essential for cognitive function, emotional regulation, and overall well-being.

- **Cognitive Benefits:** Sleep plays a crucial role in memory consolidation, problem-solving, and critical thinking. Lack of sleep can lead to impaired judgement and increased irritability.
- **Emotional Regulation:** Adequate sleep helps regulate emotions and stress

responses. Poor sleep can heighten anxiety and lead to negative thinking patterns.

### 2. Nutrition: Fueling the Brain

What you eat significantly impacts your mental clarity and cognitive function.

- **Balanced Diet:** A diet rich in whole foods, including fruits, vegetables, whole grains, lean proteins, and healthy fats, provides essential nutrients that support brain health.
- **Hydration:** Staying hydrated is vital for cognitive performance. Dehydration can lead to fatigue, difficulty concentrating, and mood swings. Aim to drink plenty of water throughout the day.
- **Limit Processed Foods:** Reduce consumption of sugary and highly processed foods, as they can lead to energy crashes and hinder mental clarity.

### 3. Exercise: The Mind-Body Connection

Physical activity is one of the most effective ways to enhance mental clarity.

- **Endorphin Release:** Exercise stimulates the release of endorphins, chemicals that promote feelings of happiness and reduce stress. Regular physical activity can boost overall mood and cognitive function.
- **Increased Blood Flow:** Exercise enhances blood circulation, delivering oxygen and nutrients to the brain. This increase in blood flow improves cognitive function, focus, and memory.
- **Stress Reduction:** Regular exercise can help mitigate stress and anxiety, providing a sense of accomplishment and boosting confidence.

# Overcoming Setbacks

Setbacks are an inevitable part of life, and learning to navigate them is crucial for personal growth and mental clarity. Whether you're grappling with overthinking or facing challenges in other areas, understanding how to handle relapses, learn from failures, and celebrate progress can empower you to overcome obstacles and foster resilience.

## How to Handle Relapses into Overthinking

Relapses into overthinking can be disheartening, but they are a common experience. The key is to approach these moments with compassion and effective strategies.

**1. Acknowledge Your Feelings:**

Recognizing and accepting your feelings of overthinking is the first step toward overcoming them.

- **Self-Compassion:** Be kind to yourself. Understand that setbacks are a natural part of the process. Remind yourself that everyone experiences moments of doubt and anxiety.
- **Identify Triggers:** Take note of what may have triggered your relapse. Was it a stressful event, a particular thought, or a specific environment? Understanding your triggers can help you prepare for future challenges.

**2. Use Mindfulness Techniques:**

Mindfulness practices can help you regain control over your thoughts.

- **Grounding Exercises:** Engage in grounding techniques such as deep breathing, focusing on your surroundings, or using your senses to anchor yourself in the present moment. This practice can help reduce anxiety and break the cycle of overthinking.
- **Thought Observation:** Instead of trying to suppress your thoughts, observe them without judgement. Recognize them as temporary and separate from your identity. This awareness can diminish their power.

### 3. Reframe Your Thoughts:

Challenging negative thought patterns is essential for breaking free from overthinking.

- **Cognitive Restructuring:** Identify negative thoughts and reframe them into more constructive ones. For example, if you think, "I always mess things up," reframe it to, "I've faced challenges before, and I can learn from this."

- **Limit Catastrophizing:** When you find yourself imagining the worst-case scenario, take a step back. Ask yourself, "What's the evidence for this thought?" and "What's a more realistic outcome?" This practice can help reduce anxiety.

**4. Take Action:**

Sometimes, taking small, actionable steps can help combat overthinking.

- **Set Achievable Goals:** Break down your tasks into manageable steps. Focus on completing one small task at a time to regain a sense of control and accomplishment.
- **Limit Decision-Making:** If overthinking is tied to decision-making, simplify your choices. Set clear parameters for decisions and stick to them, reducing the cognitive load.

# Learning from Failure and Moving Forward

Failure can be a powerful teacher, offering valuable lessons that can lead to personal growth and resilience.

**1. Embrace a Growth Mindset:**

Adopting a growth mindset allows you to view failure as an opportunity for growth.

- **Reframe Failure:** Instead of viewing failure as a reflection of your worth, see it as a stepping stone to success. Ask yourself what you can learn from the experience and how it can inform your future actions.
- **Focus on Effort Over Outcome:** Shift your focus from the end result to the effort you put in. Recognize that persistence and resilience are key components of success.

**2. Reflect on the Experience:**

Taking time to reflect on failures can deepen your understanding and inform your future decisions.

- **Journaling:** Write about your experience, exploring what went wrong and what you could have done differently. This process of reflection can provide clarity and insight.
- **Seek Feedback:** Consider seeking feedback from trusted friends or mentors. They can offer valuable perspectives that you may not have considered.

3. Develop an Action Plan:

Use your reflections to create a clear action plan moving forward.

- **Set Specific Goals:** Based on your reflections, establish specific, achievable goals for improvement. Make sure these goals are measurable so you can track your progress.
- **Identify Resources:** Determine what resources, skills, or support you might

need to achieve your goals. This could include seeking mentorship, enrolling in courses, or building a support network.

## Celebrating Your Progress

Celebrating progress, no matter how small, is vital for maintaining motivation and reinforcing positive habits.

1. Acknowledge Achievements:

Take time to recognize and celebrate your accomplishments.

- **Create Milestones:** Break your larger goals into smaller milestones and celebrate each achievement. This could be as simple as treating yourself to something enjoyable or sharing your success with others.
- **Use Positive Reinforcement:** Reward yourself for completing tasks or overcoming challenges. This positive

reinforcement encourages continued progress.

**2. Keep a Success Journal:**

Documenting your successes helps reinforce your progress.

- **Daily or Weekly Entries:** Write about your accomplishments, lessons learned, and moments of clarity. This journal serves as a reminder of your journey and can be particularly helpful during challenging times.
- **Reflect on Growth:** Periodically review your journal to see how far you've come. Reflecting on your progress can provide motivation and remind you of your resilience.

**3. Share Your Journey:**

Sharing your experiences with others can deepen your sense of connection and accountability.

- **Join Support Groups:** Consider joining groups focused on personal development,

mental health, or specific challenges you face. Sharing your journey with others fosters connection and provides mutual support.
- **Inspire Others:** Share your story, whether through social media, blogging, or speaking engagements. Your experiences may resonate with others and encourage them in their journeys.

# Daily Mindfulness Prompts

1. **Morning Reflections:**
   - What am I feeling right now, and why?
   - What intention do I want to set for today?
   - What is one thing I am grateful for as I start my day?
   - How can I show kindness to myself today?
2. **Evening Reflections:**
   - What was the most peaceful moment of my day?

- What did I learn about myself today?
- What am I proud of accomplishing today?
- How can I let go of stress or negative emotions before bed?
- What went well today, and how did I contribute to it?

---

## Prompts for Emotional Awareness

3. **Exploring Emotions:**
    - What emotion am I feeling right now, and what triggered it?
    - How does my body feel when I experience strong emotions?
    - What is one thing I can do to honour and accept my emotions today?
    - What are my emotional needs at this moment?

- When was the last time I felt at peace? What contributed to that feeling?
4. **Understanding Negative Emotions:**
   - What recurring negative thoughts do I notice in my mind?
   - What can I do to address these thoughts without judgement?
   - What is my go-to reaction to stress, and how can I mindfully shift that response?

---

# Prompts for Gratitude

5. **Gratitude Awareness:**
   - List three things you are grateful for today and why.
   - How does gratitude shift my mindset and mood?
   - Who in my life am I grateful for, and how have they impacted me?
   - What small moments today brought me joy or comfort?

- How can I incorporate more gratitude into my daily routine?

## Prompts for Self-Awareness and Reflection

6. **Understanding Myself:**
    - What are three things I love about myself?
    - What are my biggest strengths, and how do I use them in daily life?
    - How do I define success for myself, and how does it make me feel?
    - What limiting beliefs do I need to let go of to feel more fulfilled?
    - What is one habit that no longer serves me, and how can I release it?
7. **Recognizing Personal Growth:**
    - In what areas of my life have I grown the most recently?
    - What challenges have shaped me into a stronger person?

- How have my priorities shifted in the last year?
- What am I most proud of achieving, and what did I learn from the journey?
- How do I handle stress now compared to in the past?

---

## Prompts for Staying Present

8. **Mindfulness in the Present Moment:**
    - What sights, sounds, and smells do I notice around me right now?
    - How does my body feel at this moment? Am I carrying tension anywhere?
    - What is one thing I can do to slow down and be present in this moment?
    - What's something I've been overlooking today, and how can I appreciate it?

- How does it feel to pause and breathe mindfully?

## Prompts for Mindful Breathing and Grounding

9. **Breath Awareness:**
    - When was the last time I focused on my breath? How did it make me feel?
    - How can I incorporate mindful breathing into my day-to-day routine?
    - What changes do I notice in my body and mind after taking five deep breaths?
    - What distractions arise when I try to focus on my breathing, and how do I bring myself back?
    - How can I practise mindfulness when I feel overwhelmed?

## Prompts for Stress and Anxiety Management

10. **Releasing Stress:**
    - What is currently causing me the most stress, and how am I handling it?
    - What are three things I can do to reduce stress in my life today?
    - How does my body react to stress, and what can I do to release that tension?
    - What am I holding onto that is no longer serving me, and how can I let it go?
    - When do I feel most at peace, and how can I cultivate more of that feeling?
11. **Managing Anxiety:**
    - What fears or anxieties have been on my mind recently, and are they realistic?
    - What grounding techniques can I use when I start feeling anxious?

- How do I typically respond to anxiety, and what mindful actions can help shift that response?
- What thoughts do I need to challenge to reduce my anxiety?
- How can I show compassion to myself when I feel overwhelmed?

---

## Prompts for Personal Intentions and Goals

12. **Setting Intentions:**
    - What is one thing I want to accomplish this week, and why is it important to me?
    - What intention do I want to set for this month, and how can I align my actions with it?
    - How can I live more in line with my core values today?
    - What is one mindful habit I can introduce to my life, and how can I stay consistent?

- What distractions do I need to let go of to focus on my goals?

13. **Mindful Goal-Setting:**
    - What goals truly matter to me, and why do they align with my values?
    - How can I set more realistic goals that won't overwhelm me?
    - What small steps can I take today toward my long-term goals?
    - What mental roadblocks are preventing me from achieving my goals?
    - How can I celebrate small successes along the way?

---

# Prompts for Relationships and Connections

14. **Mindful Communication:**
    - How can I listen more attentively during conversations?
    - What relationships in my life need more mindful attention?

- How can I express gratitude toward someone today?
- What does being present in my relationships mean to me, and how can I embody that?
- How do I want to show up for the people I care about?

15. **Navigating Conflict Mindfully:**
    - What recurring conflicts have I been overthinking, and how can I approach them mindfully?
    - How do I typically react during conflict, and how can I respond with more patience?
    - How can I create more space for open, non-judgmental communication in my relationships?
    - What emotional triggers come up during conflict, and how can I work through them?
    - How can I practise empathy and understanding in challenging conversations?

## Prompts for Self-Love and Compassion

16. **Practising Self-Compassion:**
    - How have I been kind to myself recently?
    - What does self-love look like for me today?
    - How can I be more gentle with myself during difficult times?
    - What critical thoughts about myself do I need to release, and how can I replace them with kindness?
    - How can I practise unconditional love for myself, flaws and all?

17. **Accepting Imperfections:**
    - What imperfections in myself do I struggle to accept, and why?
    - How can I let go of the need for perfection today?

- What negative self-talk do I want to replace with more encouraging words?
- What have my perceived imperfections taught me about resilience and growth?
- How can I practise gratitude for my unique journey and self?

## Prompts for Letting Go and Moving Forward

18. **Letting Go of the Past:**
    - What am I holding onto from the past that no longer serves me?
    - How can I forgive myself for past mistakes and move forward?
    - What lessons have I learned from past challenges that I can apply to my present?
    - How does holding onto old emotions affect my current mindset?

- How can I gently release regret and focus on the present moment?
19. **Moving Forward:**
    - What is one thing I can do to move forward from a difficult experience?
    - How can I practise mindfulness to embrace change?
    - What new opportunities are opening up for me right now?
    - How can I practise patience and trust the process of growth?
    - What does moving forward with grace and self-compassion look like to me?

---

## Prompts for Mindful Living

20. **Embracing Life Fully:**
    - How can I savour small moments of joy today?
    - What routines or habits help me feel grounded and connected to the present moment?

- How can I live with more purpose and intention this week?
- What does it mean to live mindfully, and how can I apply that to my life?
- How can I infuse mindfulness into mundane tasks and daily routines?

**Overthinker's Bible**

**Overthinker's Bible**

Printed in Great Britain
by Amazon